Changing World,
Unchanging Church?

Changing World,
Unchanging Church?

An Agenda for Christians in Public Life

Edited by David Clark

MOWBRAY

Mowbray
A Cassell imprint
Wellington House, 125 Strand, London WC2R 0BB
PO Box 605, Herndon, VA 20172

First published 1997

British Library Cataloguing-in-Publication Data
A catalogue record for this book is available from the British Library.

ISBN 0-264-67421-9

See p. 129 for further information on the copyright of pp. 127–9.

Typeset by Fakenham Photosetting Limited, Fakenham, Norfolk
Printed and bound in Great Britain by J. W. Arrowsmith Ltd, Bristol

Contents

Introduction
Changing world – but unchanging church?   David Clark   1

I. Changing religion   13

1. Fundamental issues   14
The earth as a created community   Edward Echlin   15
The poor are our agenda   Michael Taylor   17
Choices at the heart of technology   Ruth Conway   21
Market wisdom or market mayhem?   Mostyn Davies   25
Beyond Laurel and Hardy   John Kennedy   28
Christian women in public life – leaven for a new culture? (1)
    Mary Grey   30
Learning communities   David Clark   32
Responding to a culture in crisis   John Austin   35

2. A new kind of faith   38
Reflections of a Christian humanist   Helen Oppenheimer   39
Spirituality on the super-highway   Peter Challen and colleagues   42
The power of the Kingdom   David Clark   44
Gardens and cities   Rowan Williams   48
Christian women in public life – leaven for a new culture? (2)
    Mary Grey   51
The Gospel as public truth   Lesslie Newbigin   53

3. The great divide   56
A public vision for society   George Carey   57
Christians in public life: the theological challenge
    Alistair McFadyen   60
The churches and public affairs   Andrew Purkis   63
The two cultures   Lois Green   66
The search   David Clark   69

4. A new kind of mission   72
Models of mission   David Clark   73

Models of mission – transformation   David Clark   75
The journey in and the journey out   David Clark   78
Mission as dialogue   Kevin Walcot   81
Doing theology in public life   Elizabeth Templeton   85

II. Changing church   89

5. The vocation of the People of God   90
Lay vocation – the call to becoming persons   David Clark   91
Theology and the human city   Martin Stringer   94
The prophetic tradition in the contemporary world   John Davies   96

6. The missionary structure of the congregation   101
Engaging in mission – the church as a 'learning organization'
David Clark   102
Ministry in the world – the role of the local church   Dick Wolff   106
Worship which frees and unites   Dick Wolff   109
A spirituality for Christians in public life   Gerard Hughes   113
Theological auditing   Peter Challen   115
Everyday ethics: where do we begin?   Richard Jones   117
The local church at work – triggers for awareness-raising
Gill College   119

7. The missionary structure of the institution   122
The Portsmouth Faith and Work Project – raising questions
Ann Leonard   123
Faith and work Guildford-style   David Welbourn   125
Faith and work consultations in the Diocese of Rochester
Garth Norman and Gordon Oliver   126
Resource groups – a project   Rachel Jenkins   127
Faith, lifestyle and membership of the Christian church
Sue Clark   130
Industrial Mission – future perspectives   Rowland Goodwin   133
Ministry in secular employment (MSE)   Michael Ranken   136
The role of church leaders – a neglected ministry?
Michael Henshall   138

III. Changing society   143

8. Personal perspectives   144
Politics and faith   Hilary Armstrong   145
Faith and politics – a personal reflection   Alistair Burt   146
... also God's children?   Evelyn Jones   148
True and fair   Alison Lusty   149

Towards quality of service   David Pinwell   150
Councillor who …?   Andrew Coulson   151
Train – or no tomorrow   Kathleen Carey   152
Issues of integrity   Malcolm Claydon   154
Faith in the inner city   Janette Stebbens   155
'Light in a dark place'?   Paul Cooper   156
The school – a community of work and worth   Sue Gibbons   158
At the 'crossroads'   Ruth Stables   159

9. Societal perspectives   163
Taxation not donation   Paul Nicolson   164
Christian perspectives on the social audit of commercial companies
    Richard Adams   167
Beyond public fundamentalism – a ministry in waiting
    David Clark   169
Christian thought and action in public education   Jack Priestley   173
Social work and public life   Howard Tripp   177
Christian responses to a Health Service in transition
    James Woodward   179
Forgiveness in public life   Brian Frost   182

Conclusion
    David Clark   185

References   196

Introduction
David Clark

CHANGING WORLD – BUT UNCHANGING CHURCH?

The end of a millennium may be something of a chronological gimmick but it does help to concentrate the mind. For most people in our society it is an opportunity to plan symbolic events and create symbolic monuments, though of a dominantly secular not sacred kind.

For Christians, however, the year AD 2000 provides an opportunity to reflect not only on human achievements, for what they are, but on God's purposes for his world and his church. And here the overriding question is whether we are any nearer understanding the true nature of his Kingdom, and have over the past millennium moved any nearer to making it a reality on earth as in heaven.

Of one thing we can be certain; that change, and a mind-blowing rapidity of change, is now the norm. The twentieth century has been one of incredible development across the world scene. My father, who was born in 1897, has in his life-time witnessed a scientific revolution, giving us the power to sustain or obliterate human life; a demographic revolution, witnessing both a huge rise in the world's population and vastly increased life-expectancy; a technological revolution, bringing instantaneous communication and high-speed travel across the entire globe; an economic revolution, offering to billions a state of physical well-being and material affluence beyond the wildest dreams of earlier generations; a cultural revolution in which the deep desire to retain social roots vies with an ever-encroaching transformation of life-styles and norms; and an ecological revolution, which has opened the planet to human use or abuse in a quite terrifying way. So it is something of an understatement to say that we are part of a 'changing world'.

But if such epoch-making developments have been transforming the life of our society, what of the church? As one of the great channels of God's grace, how has it fared over this century of vastly accelerating change? What lessons have been learnt about the nature of the Kingdom, and how can those who call themselves Christians continue to be the means by which it becomes more real and meaningful for all men and women? Here our immediate response is largely restricted to that fragment of the world (England) which is our home, and to that period through which we have lived (the second half of the twentieth century). But as our planet shrinks and experiences, insights and resources traverse the globe at ever-increasing speed, we believe that important aspects of what is happening in our neck of the woods will have considerable significance elsewhere.

The twentieth century has seen the structures of the church in England change more slowly than within any other institution. Whereas education, health and welfare, industry and commerce, government itself and, that once bastion of cultural norms, the family, are almost unrecognizable from a century ago, the church as an organization appears to have altered little. Its buildings, despite the odd adjacent temple or mosque, still dominate the skyline of villages and towns, as well as a good number of cities; its worship services are still held at the traditional times; rites of passage are still celebrated therein by many; its ministers are still recognized by their formal attire; and its denominational brands and varieties remain much as they appeared at the outset of the century.

But the problem with a 'changing world' and an 'unchanging church' is that the two risk drawing 'worlds apart'. There are those who argue that the church in England is not there to be the blazer of trails, but the guardian of the faith. It exists to point, as its spires still remind us, to things eternal, essentially unchanging. Its task is not to let the world set the agenda, but to go on reminding us of our human roots yet eternal destiny as decreed by Scripture and tradition.

But if any institution, even a sacred institution, gradually loses contact with the people it is meant to serve; if its symbols become increasingly meaningless and its rituals outmoded; if it ceases to communicate effectively with up and coming generations; and if it thus 'ages' in every sense: then it must in time be threatened with extinction.

THE CAPTIVITY OF THE CHURCH

As a new millennium approaches, the institutional church in England would seem to be nearing that terminal state. It has become caught in a time-warp out of which it finds it almost impossible to escape. Thus, far from being the preserver of the faith of a nation, it becomes ever more like a cultural museum which people visit to remind them of a nostalgic past, but which seems to have little to say to the present or offer to the future.

Six features appear to hold the church captive (Clark, 1984) to this anachronistic situation; six 'isms' which, the more absolute they become, the more they cut the church off from a changing world:

- *Clericalism.* The domination of the ordained ministry (with powerful male overtones) in leadership and decision-making, deskills and domesticates the laity.

- *Parochialism.* Preoccupation with the needs of the local neighbourhood, as community of place, channels the church's energies away from communities of interest and communities of concern.
- *Congregationalism.* Many church members only meet once a Sunday and then have little time or inclination to engage on a personal level with one another. The form has replaced the substance of human encounter.
- *Denominationalism.* A divided church is living with a massive duplication of plant and personnel which compels it to be concerned far more with sectarian survival than its corporate mission.
- *Secularism.* The secularistic culture of society is increasingly marginalizing or colonizing the sacred symbols, rituals and, above all, values and beliefs which previous generations took for granted.
- *Dogmatism.* On the one hand, a society dominated by secularism will not listen to messages which do not fit neatly into its restrictive constructs. But, on the other, a church dominated by the 'isms' listed above is unable to shake clear of its own dogmatic tendencies. As a consequence, there is no dialogue, so essential a process if the whole of society is to become a genuine learning and maturing community.

THE LIBERATION OF THE CHURCH

It would be naïve to pretend that even the most drastic re-ordering of the church's life and leadership would automatically liberate it to assume a meaningful and dynamic role in the next millennium. For our world is not as it was a century ago. Of all the 'isms' listed above, it is of course secularism which now presents Christian faith with its most profound challenge. The tragedy is that just as the church should be putting all its energies into a creative response to this most potent of challenges, the other 'isms' hold it captive to an outmoded past. Until and unless these latter 'isms' are addressed, the church will be forced to respond to an increasingly secular culture with its limbs shackled.

The liberation of the church for ministry and mission in the next millennium will not be a quick or simple matter. If it still has an essential part to play in the public life of society, as all Christians believe, honouring that vocation will require a determined effort to address all the 'isms' outlined above. The church will not experience a sudden transformation. The complexity and power of the captivity it is experiencing will see to that. But here and there new awakenings will come and new initiatives be taken, often on the margins and 'in the cracks' of both church and society, which will be signs of hope, seeds of liberation. These signs will embody new forms of Christian community (Clark, 1984). They will reveal new styles of leadership and a new understanding of the meaning of Christian vocation. They will embrace a new language which will enable the church once again to communicate with, as well as learn from, a society now distanced from it (Williams, 1996). They will encompass a new spirituality which offers inspiration and energy resulting from an encounter with the divine within the whole of his creation (Hughes, 1985). They will be acted parables of faith, hope and love.

One of these means of liberation, these signs of transformation, is the growing awareness that Christians, all Christians, are called to exercise their ministry not just within the church but well beyond it; not only within the private domain but in the public arena. It is with this aspect of the 're-formation' of the church for its mission in the next millennium that this book is concerned. The (re)engagement of Christians with the public life of our society will have profound implications for all the 'isms' which currently hold the church captive. Indeed it is argued by many in this book that if a new kind of engagement between Christians and wider society begins to take place, then the lethal embrace of clericalism, parochialism, congregationalism and denominationalism will be greatly weakened. A new way of being church could really become a possibility. And if such an engagement does succeed, then the domination of secularism and dogmatism will also be confronted. A new way of being church must inevitably mean a new way of being society.

DISENGAGEMENT

A reawakening of the church, the whole church, to the importance of its ministry within the public arena has, however, to be set against a century of gradual disengagement. The end of the nineteenth century witnessed a very different relationship between church and society (Hastings, 1991). Not only was the Church of England then a major player on the national stage, but Nonconformity was at its height permeating every sector of public life and very influential on the political scene (Munson, 1991). Roman Catholicism was only just emerging from centuries of social as well as religious exclusion, but was becoming steadily more influential within public affairs. The twentieth century, however, has seen all the major denominations declining, first steadily, but in recent years (Brierley and Wraight, 1995) more rapidly, in both numerical strength and overall influence on the public scene. The relatively small increase in the strength of the more charismatic and evangelical forms of churchmanship has in no way compensated for this general state of diminution and marginalization.

It is not our intention to document this century-long process of gradual disengagement nor to present a detailed analysis of the reasons for withdrawal. These have been more than adequately covered elsewhere (Gilbert, 1980; Hastings, 1991). Suffice it to say that the emergence of 'two worlds', church and society, increasingly removed from one another, was as much the result of society moving rapidly into a new cultural and secular mode as it was of the church being held captive by 'cultural lag'.

What I shall outline below is the broad sweep of attempts by the church over the second half of this century to re-engage with the public arena, leading up to the programme out of which the papers presented in this book have come.

RE-ENGAGEMENT?

The story of the church's attempted re-engagement with public life is perhaps epitomized by the foundation in 1938 of the *Iona Community* by George MacLeod, a Church of Scotland Minister. The Iona Community's early *raison d'être* was the search for a new understanding of the meaning and purpose of work in a society which, in the mid-1930s, had sent six million men on to the dole queues. Since its foundation, the Community (based both in Glasgow and on the Island of Iona, where the rebuilding of the Abbey as an acted parable of a new society in the making was completed in 1966) has exercised an influence out of all proportion to its actual membership. But as our focus is on the English scene, we will in what follows remain south of the border.

In 1944, Bishop Leslie Hunter set up in Sheffield what came to be known as an '*Industrial Mission*', led by the dynamic figure of Ted Wickham. Since that time, Industrial Mission has been one of the most significant models of the church's attempt to re-engage with the world of work. Industrial Mission gradually spread across the country, linking up with other denominational endeavours in the same mould, notably the work of Methodism's Bill Gowland and the Luton Industrial College, founded in 1954. The 1960s saw Industrial Mission in some disarray over its relationship with the wider church, not least in Sheffield itself (Bagshaw, 1994), but it weathered the storm and has continued exercising an impressive ministry to the present day.

Industrial Mission's slowly declining influence, however, would now be acknowledged by all involved (*Industrial Mission*, 1988). Three main reasons for this seem clear. First, the changing nature of modern society, with the disappearance of huge tracts of the 'manual' industries such as steel and coal-mining, and the emergence of a high-tech world in which knowledge and automation are the keys to the future. Secondly, the declining economic as well as numerical strength of the churches (not least, of late, the Church of England), and increasing pressure to withdraw clergy from extra-parochial ministries. And, thirdly, a growing awareness that the engagement of the church with the world of work cannot rely on a dwindling number of ordained ministers operating a chaplaincy model, however committed and dedicated to their task.

Another important attempt during this period to bring Christian faith to bear on the public arena was that of the *laity centres* (Clark, 1987, pp. 165–8). These have taken a wide variety of forms, sometimes reflecting aspects of the German lay academies established soon after the Second World War. Pre-eminent in this context was the William Temple College founded in 1947 at Hawarden near Chester, and which moved to Rugby in the early 1950s. Under its dynamic Principal, Mollie Batten, the William Temple College for two decades and more pioneered one of the most creative training centres for the engagement of church and society witnessed on the English scene this century. The many hundreds of those, mostly lay people, who passed through its doors bear witness to its mature attempt to bring a living faith to bear on the realities of the contemporary world. It is a sad commentary on the inability of church and society to stay in touch that the college closed a few years after Mollie Batten retired in 1966. In 1971, its assets were translated into the William Temple Foundation, now based in Manchester, which has very effectively sustained certain aspects of the work of the college, but inevitably on a much narrower front.

Other 'laity centres' sprang up in the years following the Second World War, some providing excellent conferences and courses for Christians seeking to gain a deeper understanding of the relation between faith and the modern world. But their number has been relatively few, their programmes have focused on 'religious' as much as 'secular' issues, and they too have struggled to remain solvent in a declining 'market', opening their facilities to many secular organizations and agencies simply to balance the budget. Their sometimes strong denominational affiliations have also meant a certain narrowness in the range of participants attending them.

During the 1960s, there were other attempts to grasp the nettle of *lay vocation* in the public arena and to set up training programmes to help prepare people for this call. A World Council of Churches growing in energy and influence boosted this movement with its study of 'the missionary structure of the congregation' (for example, Williams, 1963, 1964). The English champion of the lay role in this task was Mark Gibbs who, with Ralph Morton, in 1964 wrote his seminal *God's Frozen People*. From 1966, the Audenshaw Foundation, set up by Mark Gibbs, produced a series of Audenshaw Papers focusing on lay ministry in the public domain. In 1971, Gibbs' and Morton's second book, *God's Lively People*, followed.

A number of denominations sought to build such developments into their ongoing life, not least Methodism which in the 1960s set up a Board of Lay Training under Pauline Webb. The Church of England pursued a similar line largely on a diocesan basis, often associated with its growing number of conference and retreat centres.

The 1970s, however, saw the renewed missionary impetus in the public arena beginning to falter. The visionary energy of the 1960s seemed to seep away, perhaps in part undermined by the rough waters into which the ecumenical movement was now sailing. Clerical interests and concerns seemed to reassert themselves as continuing decline, not least economic, began to thrust the denominations back into their shells. The courses and conferences for laity at work got lost in more religious agendas, not least the quest for 'spirit-led' (charismatic) and private expressions of faith.

However, a different approach by the churches to re-engage with a secular society, albeit somewhat unintentionally, gathered momentum in the 1960s and did retain its momentum thereafter. *Non-stipendiary ministry* (priests earning their living from a secular occupation whilst serving the institutional church in an unpaid capacity) had been on and off the Church of England's agenda for some decades (Vaughan, 1990). But in 1960, the Southwark Ordination Course was established to enable men to train for the priesthood on a part-time basis whilst remaining in their secular occupations. This gradually became a model for other courses throughout the country. From our perspective, the importance of this initiative was that a good proportion of those trained were encouraged to exercise their calling through continued full-time employment in mainstream society. In the Church of England, those who retained a work-focused priority in their vocation came to be known as 'ministers in secular employment' (MSE), rather than as 'non-stipendiary ministers' whose ministry was related primarily to the parish church.

In the late 1960s, Methodism formally followed suit when its Commission on the Church's Ministry in the Modern World recommended the creation of 'sector ordained ministry', the 'secondment' of ordained ministers to secular posts both to earn their full-time living there as well as to represent the church in the public domain. Of the other denominations, the URC has most actively backed this kind of development.

MSE, or sector ministry, did not adopt a chaplaincy model. It was about men (and later women) being ordained as focal points of Christian engagement with secular institutions which might otherwise have continued to drift further and further away from any form of contact with the church. It has remained a form of ministry which has had ambiguous support. It never received the enthusiastic backing of the church as a whole. There has always been a feeling amongst more traditional clergy and laity that it falls short of the 'proper' calling of an ordained minister which is to have liturgical and pastoral responsibility for a local congregation. Nor have MSEs and sector ministers found it easy to 'report back' to the church in any effective way. They have, however, gained mutual support through the setting up of their own associations (the Methodist one fading out after a time, but the Anglican one, CHRISM, ecumenical in interest and ongoing).

One other means by which the church has sought to affirm the importance of Christian involvement in the public arena has had a history somewhat longer than the period with which we are dealing. For many decades the (largely Anglican) Evangelical Alliance and the Roman Catholic Church have encouraged the formation of 'fellowships' or 'sodalities' made up of those with a similar occupational background. The Nurses' Christian Fellowship (Evangelical) and the Catenian Association (Roman Catholic businessmen) are but two examples amongst many. The problem with these and many similar associations has been twofold. First, that they have a relatively restrictive theological base, only attracting lay people of like religious persuasion. Secondly, that they remain very much 'come structures', associations for mutual support and encouragement, rather than 'go structures', groups actively concerned to equip their members to engage as Christians with non-Christians around issues of common concern. Nonetheless, these groups and networks provide an important organizational model from which lessons can be learned with regard to the church's future engagement with public life.

The history of the church in England in its attempts to re-engage with a rapidly changing society has not been an outstanding success. Some of those ventures mentioned above have made a noteworthy contribution though on a limited regional or time scale. But, from the point of view of a deliberate and sustainable corporate policy of engagement, no denomination had made any significant new impact up to the mid 1980s.

A NEW ERA?

Whether or not it was the Thatcher years which spurred the churches into action once again is hard to say. Certainly her policies led to the politicization of many of those who had never before faced questions about Christian faith and contemporary values. Or whether the continuing numerical decline, as well as ageing membership of the churches, suddenly brought home to at least some that re-engagement with a secular culture was an imperative for survival, is difficult to assess. But between 1985 and 1990 four noteworthy denominational publications on the church's ministry in the public domain saw the light of day.

In 1985, a working party of the General Synod Board of Education produced a symposium of essays addressing the question of 'what problems prevent lay people of today's Church of England from exercising more effectively their vocation, their calling from God, to be the people of God in the Church and the world' (*All Are Called*, 1985). Two years later, a report of the same Board along similar lines was presented to the General Synod for reflection and action (*Called to be Adult Disciples*, 1987). Meanwhile the Roman Catholic Synod of Bishops meeting in Rome in 1987 had been focusing on much the same theme. In the ensuing Apostolic Exhortation *Christifideles Laici* (1989), much of the impressive material from the bishops' meeting found public expression in the UK as elsewhere. Then, in 1990, the Methodist Church published its own report on the role of the lay Christian in today's world entitled *The Ministry of the People of God in the World.* Add to these documents two very large conferences in 1991, the Rerum Novarum Centenary Conference (celebrating the papal encyclical of that name promulgated a century ago) and the Malvern Conference (50 years after the famous Malvern Conference of 1941), and the scene seemed at last set for a possible new era in church–society relations, not least with regard to the role of the 'ordinary Christian' in public life.

CHRISTIANS IN PUBLIC LIFE (CIPL)

It was against the background of this reappraisal and attempted relaunch of lay vocation in the modern world, that Christians in Public Life, out of which have come the position papers that make up this book, was established.

The 'home' of this programme was Westhill College, a Free Church foundation training teachers, community and youth workers, and church leaders, located in Birmingham, and a member of the Selly Oak Colleges Federation. Westhill College has always had a commitment to lay ministry through the professions for which it trains students, as well as on a wider canvas. But in 1991 its new Principal, Dr Jack Priestley, decided to revisit this commitment and asked me, as a member of staff, to explore how the college might give it fuller expression.

A round of conversations across the country in the summer of 1991 met a ready response to the suggestion of setting up some kind of base at Westhill to service a loose network of individuals and associations working to further Christian faith in the public domain. A consultation at Westhill attended by some sixty people in September 1991 confirmed this initiative. Thus began Christians in Public Life (CIPL). On 2 March 1992, the Archbishop of Canterbury visited the Selly Oak Colleges and with his co-operation the opportunity was found to build the official launch of CIPL into his schedule.

Westhill College agreed that part of my time at the college would be made available to act as Co-ordinator of the programme. I have received over the years since 1992 considerable help on a voluntary basis, first from Sister Jo Chambers SND, and then from Sister Maureen Connor ra, acting as Assistant Co-ordinators. Carole Surtees has served as a very efficient Administrative Secretary. The programme has received the ongoing support of a strong Steering Committee on which have served a number of influential representatives of all the major denominations.* A national network of 'development

---

* The present members of CIPL's Steering Committee are Dr Jack Priestley (Chair), Sister Kathleen Bulley SND, Martin Conway, Canon Denis Claringbull, Valerie Evans, Lois Green, Bishop Michael Henshall, Revd Christina le Moignan, Revd Brian Nicholls, Revd Deirdre Palk, Bishop Howard Tripp, Revd Elizabeth Welch, Leonora Wilson. Yvonne Craig, Revd Donald Eadie, Revd Eric Lord, Sister Margaret McHard, Hilary Ineson and the Revd Simon Oxley have also served as members.

workers' has also acted voluntarily as CIPL's ears and eyes on the regional scene.

THE PROGRAMME

The purpose and aims of CIPL have been set out as follows:

> To achieve a new quality of public life by enabling Christians to engage, share and work together with others in addressing fundamental issues of common concern by:

1. Raising the awareness of Christians to the fact that engagement in public life is an an essential part of mission.
2. Assisting the church to provide worship, education and pastoral care which will empower Christians for their engagement in public life.
3. Developing ways by which the experience and skills of Christians in public life can help equip the church for its contemporary task.
4. Bringing the resources of Christian faith to bear on society through the life and work of Christians active within all sectors of society.
5. Bringing secular agencies to a realization that Christian insights have an essential contribution to make to sustaining their integrity, well-being and long-term effectiveness.
6. Forging new partnerships between Christians and others concerned about the future health and well-being of our society.

CIPL has sought to implement this programme in three main ways:

*   A range of 'position papers' (to which we return below).
*   A number of day consultations and two national residential conferences around faith and public life issues.
*   Research into the experiences of Christians at work and at church (Clark, 1993). This was the first ever survey of its kind, asking nearly four hundred Christians of all denominations to respond to questions about their ministry in the workplace, and about how effectively they felt their church was supporting them in this task. The good news was that the large majority of respondents had a strong sense of Christian vocation in their working lives. The bad news was that most of them received little help in fulfilling this vocation from the worship, pastoral care or educational activities of their local church.

However, perhaps the most important contributions of CIPL so far to the task of a recoupling of church and society has been through its position papers. At the time of writing, 131 have been published.

The position papers were commissioned to help set an agenda for the church in the public arena. They were meant to express the author's personal view as to what was of current concern in public life, what light faith might throw on the issues identified, what implications the insights gained might have for church and society, and what changes might therefore be called for in both arenas. They were purposely brief (usually two printed sides of A4) to facilitate assimilation and dissemination. A curriculum vitae at the end of each article indicated the role of the author at the time of writing.

The position papers were grouped into a form of curriculum (or agenda) with the following broad headings:

Overview and analysis (theological)
Ethics and issues
People (especially the views of Christians in public life)
Sectors (such as education, health, industry, etc.)
The church – roles and relationships
The church – functions and organization
Resource sheets (information and ideas to help put theory into practice)

Those people who subscribed to the position papers became 'Associates' of CIPL. Many others, who simply wanted to be kept in touch with the programme as a whole, were mailed with a newsletter.

The agenda set by these position papers has not remained merely an academic exercise. In 1994, CIPL decided to test out many of the insights and suggestions in a real life situation – that of the City of Birmingham. Thus, in January 1995, the Human City Initiative was launched to employ more effectively the resources of the Christian community to help create, develop and sustain Birmingham as a human city. The Initiative has developed a unique framework to network Christians, with others sharing their concern for the humanity of institutional life, and to support them in the public arena. The Human City Initiative ends in 1997 but plans are now afoot to set up a Human City Institute, 'owned' by a consortium of Christian and other agencies active on the Birmingham scene, to take the Initiative into a second phase. Many of CIPL's more recent position papers (not reproduced in this book) have focused on the theme of the human city. It is hoped to publish a complementary volume in due course describing the story of the Human City Initiative itself and a selection of these papers.

The current volume contains position papers written between the commencement of CIPL early in 1992 and the summer of 1996, but in the main excluding those written specifically with the Human City Initiative in mind. The papers have been produced by many eminent as well as 'ordinary' people.

Put together, these papers make up a unique and powerful commentary on the relationship of the church and the wider world at the turn of the millennium. We believe that the experiences, insights and, not least, passion revealed in these papers speak for themselves, beginning to map out a new way of being church for a new way of being society in deeper accord with the purposes of the Kingdom of God.

David Clark is a Methodist minister, an honorary research fellow on the staff of Westhill College, Birmingham, and Co-ordinator of Christians in Public Life.

PART I

Changing religion

The Christian, along with those of all other faiths and convictions, enters a new millennium with many fundamental issues to address. This section identifies some of those at the very top of the agenda and examines the kind of faith needed to respond meaningfully to these. The nature of the 'great divide' which has increasingly marginalized the Christian in public life seeking to make this faith response a reality is described, together with a new approach to mission which could help to bridge this widening gulf.

Fundamental issues

The declared purpose of the Christians in Public Life Programme is 'to achieve a new quality of public life by enabling Christians to engage, share and work together with others in addressing fundamental issues of common concern'.

The papers in this first section raise a range of such fundamental issues. They embrace actual issues of life or death (environment); 'heaven or hell' (as Channel Four's television series in 1995 described the new technology: Harrison, 1995); wealth or poverty (economics), justice or injustice (citizenship); and community or chaos (culture).

These papers also address fundamental issues of 'common' concern. They are not about 'religious' or 'secular' questions but concerns which all of us face as we search for a new world order able to sustain a rich quality of life into the next millennium. That Christians are identifying these issues with both perception and passion indicates that they lie at the very heart of God's Kingdom here and now, and yet still to come on earth.

The earth as a created community

Edward Echlin

Unless and until people live sustainably and at peace with the soil community of this earth, the human future on this planet is ambiguous.

The central, because pervasive, challenge to humanity today is the disintegration, under human impact, of the fragile surface of planet earth (Echlin, 1989; 1992). The ecological crisis is an inclusive crisis: all other problems such as inflation, sexism, poverty, overpopulation, militarism, maldistribution, war and peace, and migrations – all these are related to the environment. Unless and until people live sustainably and at peace within the soil community of this earth, the human future on this planet is ambiguous. What people call 'Gaia', the earth as a living entity, will survive and continue, complex life will evolve anew – but the human species may vanish from this earth before its due time.

For the myriad creatures on this earth are an interdependent community, every living being, from bacteria to walrus, is a soil organism dependent for its continuance on the healthy functioning of the entire community. If we can recover this realization of our shared fragility, that the beings on this earth are, under God, an interdependent community, we may be able to heal the earth and transmit healthy habitats to our children.

PEOPLE AND RESOURCES

The problem is that modern men and women, impressed by modern technology, often divide the earth into two categories – people, and resources for people's benefits. Our fellow creatures are regarded not as inherently precious in themselves, but resources for human consumption. These creatures, moreover, are widely regarded as inexhaustible, in what is called 'the infinite resources illusion'.

Because we suffer from this exploitative attitude towards other creatures (despite the awareness raised during the 1992 Rio Earth Summit), the earth continues to deteriorate, species become extinct at 10,000 times the natural extinction rate, forests shrink, soil erodes, cities swell, and human numbers, demands, wars and subsequent migrations outrace ecosystems. By refusing to live within the restraints under which God grants life on this frail planet, the restraints of solidarity within a fragile soil community, modern humanity is literally destroying our habitats by destroying our fellow creatures. We are suffering from what Vaclav Havel describes as the 'general inability of modern humanity to take control of its own destiny'.

People in consumer cultures are reluctant to acknowledge that our lifestyles – or aspirations – are earth destructive and that, despite our glittering technology, we have lost control of our lives, our planet, our future. We know that modern market societies are not sustainable – but addicted to consumerism. We indulge in massive reality avoidance. We repress the realization that people are not above the rest of the soil community, but interdependent within it. Avoidance of the lucidly vivid reality of our own unsustainable behaviour, our fictitious fantasy that we are carefree masters of other beings, debilitates modern humanity and prevents us from reintegrating with the rest of God's creation. We are not living as what we are meant to be – creatures under God within a wondrously diverse community with responsibility to love, nurture and share the planet with God's other creatures.

. . .

CHRISTIAN PERSPECTIVES

. . .

I therefore outline here a number of general Christian principles which could be developed further.

The first article of our creeds proclaims God as Creator of heaven and earth, of all that is not God. The whole earth – what we have described as the soil community – is God's Self-communication to God's creatures. The universe is the primary place of God's Self-disclosure.

For Christians, God's saving revelation is especially present in Jesus. Because Jesus of Nazareth is fully human, in the incarnation and redemption God enters the whole soil community 'reconciling to himself all things, whether on earth or in heaven, making peace by the blood of his cross' (Col 1.20). By our commitment to God in Jesus we are reconciled with our Creator, our selves and our fellow dependent creatures.

The future Kingdom which Jesus preached, which we preach and for which we live includes all creation, God's entire 'shining mountain'. The whole material creation, said Paul, 'will be set free from its bondage to decay and obtain the glorious liberty of the children of God' (Rom 8.21). For disciples of Jesus the future matters.

The church is the community committed to Jesus; 'Christ existing as community', said Dietrich Bonhoeffer. Because the whole of the cosmos, from stardust to micro-organisms, is within people, the conscious edge of evolution, and because people are within a soil community, all are, in some way, within the church.

The distinctive human presence within the soil community is that of God's image, a delegated royal and sacral presence under God, whereby we the people of God nurture and lead the whole creation in cosmic worship.

WHAT NEXT?

Christian faith flows into practice. The 'wealth of the living tradition', said Vatican II, 'flows into the practice and life of the believing and praying church' (Constitution on Divine Revelation, 8). The challenge for Christians in public life today is literally to heal God's earth and secure a sustainable future. This means educating ourselves and our contemporaries to the frailty and inter-dependence of all creation on this planet. It means recognizing that we are not masters of other beings, 'so-called resources', but fellow members with special responsibilities within a created soil community. All creation is bright and beautiful, 'heaven and earth' includes more than human beings, all praise God as Lord and King, all creation belongs to the soil community and indeed, in some way, to what we have described as the church soil community.

. . .

Edward Echlin is Honorary Research Fellow in theology, Trinity and All Saints College, Leeds University, and writes and lectures on Christian theology and ecology. He is a Roman Catholic.

The poor are our agenda
Michael Taylor

The growing number of the poor is one of the most grotesque facts about the real world.

I cannot imagine I need to argue that Christians in public life should take pov-erty seriously. The growing numbers of the poor is one of the most grotesque facts about the real world. Jesus makes them central to his ministry. He takes notice of them. He addresses their needs. He comes to announce good news to them. He suggests that whether we pay attention to them or not makes all the difference between heaven or hell. He teaches us to love our neighbours irres-pective of age-old enmities or racial differences, as a Samaritan once loved a Jew. He says the last will be first. He calls the poor blessed and promises them the Kingdom. They are clearly high on his agenda and God's agenda and there-fore on any Christian's agenda. Some would put them at the top.

The question is not whether to take the poor seriously but how; not whether to love our neighbour but how to do so effectively.

CAUTIONARY WORDS

Maybe we should sound three familiar notes of caution before getting to the serious stuff.

First, *charity is not enough*. At its best, of course, charity is *caritas*: the same as Christian love, and to that we must return. In common parlance, however, it means giving generously to a good cause, and when we give we expect a return on our money. We look for an immediate effect. Kindness must be done and be seen to be done. A night shelter for the homeless would count. So would blankets and medicines for refugees. So would food, shipped out from Europe for example for Africa's hungry millions. Such relief work is often necessary. It is a good thing to do as long as we are absolutely clear it will never make poverty go away. It can alleviate. It will not eliminate.

Second, *a modest life-style is not enough*. We are sometimes urged to cut down so that other people can have a bit more; to live more simply so that others can simply live. Modesty rather than extravagance doubtless becomes a Christian. Sacrifice becomes us even more, but we should not assume that giving things up will help the poor. Too few of us are likely to do it to make any great difference. What surplus we create will be mopped up by those who already have more than enough. And the power of a good example is extremely limited. The public at large is not going to catch on unless we can make a modest life-style fashionable, and fashions come and go.

Third, *evangelism is not enough*. We have to be ruthless about the argument that the more folk we convert to the Christian faith the better the place will be, and the more rapidly the numbers of the poor will decline. It is true the better we all become the better the world will be; but history suggests that most of us do not become much better. We could rejoice if more and more people become actively committed to a crusade against poverty. But that is not normally what we have in mind when we talk about evangelism in our present religious climate. Whatever the merits of evangelism, we are not likely to convert great numbers, and there is little if any sign that conversion leads to social action. Can any of us, for example, identify the Christians in our society by their radical commitment to the poor?

. . .

'NO CHANCE' SYSTEMS

I can think of four systems that do not give the poor a chance . . .

First, *war wedded to the arms trade is a system.* Aspects of it can be reasonably defended, as Christians are wont to do. And aspects of it are beyond any defence. Governments are encouraged to buy arms instead of bread. Manufacturers profit by selling arms to enemies we are about to fight. The system manifestly creates poverty, maintains it and prevents it being overcome. Africa, including Ethiopia, Mozambique, Angola, Sudan to name a few, has offered all too many examples, and Africa is not alone.

Second, *international debt is a system.* The history of the crisis goes back twenty years and is increasingly irrelevant. The fact is that whether justly or unjustly many Third World countries owe enormous sums of money to the richer nations and bankers of the First World. They owe more and pay more than they receive in aid. It is a burden on their backs. It prevents economies recovering, if recovery is the word. In order to earn the money to pay, they are forced to degrade the environment, by cutting and selling off the trees; to grow crops that sell abroad rather than grow crops that will secure food for their people...

Third, *trade is a system.* Third World countries have few things to sell: cotton, coffee, tea, copper, bananas, sugar. They need a decent price which they do not always get. They face fierce competition. They also face unfair practices like the dumping of subsidized, surplus European food on Third World markets, thereby undercutting local producers. If the poor could trade successfully, they would not need our 'charity'...

And *democracy is a system,* or rather the lack of it. All over the world poor people get little say and have little control over what happens to them. Their views are not heard. Their votes do not count. That is true for local communities, inner-city areas, minority groups, countries over-ruled by dictatorial regimes. And it is true of some of the enormously influential international institutions. We grumble that the European Community is not, to date, sufficiently democratic. Nor are many aspects of the United Nations. Nor are the transnational corporations which can have more power than governments. Nor is the World Bank or the International Monetary Fund which can decide to help a Third World country only if it accepts conditions which crucify the poor all over again. Nor is the GATT (General Agreement on Trade and Tariffs) or the MTO (Multi-Lateral Trade Organization) which may soon replace it. It is the strong and the rich who decide and, true to human nature, decide in their own favour.

...

Who has got the wit and the wisdom and the patience and the persistence and the energy and the influence, quite apart from the goodwill, to change the systems?

SIGNPOSTS

Coming back to ourselves, let me offer eight signposts for action:

1. *The conversions we need* are not to a kind of echo-chamber religion but to bringing good news to the poor – news that they will actually be pleased to hear.
2. *The charity or love that we need* is not a thoughtless generosity but a hard-headed determination to do what will actually make a difference, and that will certainly include changing the systems.
3. *The life-style that we need* may well be modest, but it must include the political obedience which learns how to use our opportunities in a democratic country to influence the decision-makers in government and industry and elsewhere in favour of the poor.
4. *The resources we need* include specialist agencies like a Christian Aid or a CAFOD or a World Development Movement or a Church Action on Poverty which see to it that not only are the poorest of the poor supported in the short term, but that we have the best advice on what public policies to fight for.
5. *The church communities we need* are ones which actually give us the impression that political discipleship is central to what the Lord requires of us, by helping us to understand it, train for it, and giving us support by practising it, and not taking up our time with less crucial in-church matters.
6. *The kind of evangelism we need* is one which will proclaim to all and sundry not where a narrow individual salvation might be found, but the truth about a world which is full of people who are all equally important, equally interesting, equally able to help each other and equally the children of God, and equally poor in so far as they are perverse and refuse to share with each other.
7. *The kind of worship we need* is worship which week by week takes us back to the beginning and on to the end: to the good news about the poor God with a full heart for an impoverished world.
8. *What we do not need* are Christians who say they care about the poor but are unwilling to take a single tentative step in the direction of political responsibility.

Michael Taylor is the Director of Christian Aid.

Choices at the heart of technology

Ruth Conway

There is ... a biblical understanding of liberation which can be set alongside the goals and expectations that have been built up around technology; there is an alternative yardstick which has
a central concern, not one's own success, but freedom for 'the other'.

...

How can Christians make a meaningful analysis that challenges the choices made
in the initial stages of a technology before its full implications are apparent? One
possibility is to draw on the approach used by Karen Lebacqz in her book *Justice
in an Unjust World*. She starts not with a generalized ideal of justice, but with the
realities of *in*justice experienced in people's lives. She uses a combination of
historical consciousness (naming and claiming the injustices in the world) and
biblical remembrance (searching for biblical stories that illumine the proper
response to such injustices). Technology can be approached in a similar way.

A LIBERATING FORCE?

...

Biblical remembrance deals with 'liberation': 'God is ... the liberator God of
the Exodus, who leads [the] people out of every kind of bondage, spiritual, political, social, and economic' (Tutu, 1983, p. 155). 'In the Gospels as read by the
oppressed, Jesus stands in the liberation tradition from the very beginning – and
self-consciously so' (Lebacqz, 1987, p. 73) There is therefore a biblical understanding of liberation which can be set alongside the goals and expectations that
have been built up around technology; there is an alternative yardstick which
has as a central concern, not one's own success, but freedom for 'the other'.

TECHNOLOGY FROM THE UNDERSIDE

...

However powerful its potential, any particular technological development is
not predetermined. It is shaped by innumerable choices and value judgements.
Who makes the decisions and in whose interests? The biblical story is a challenge to hear the stories of those on the underside of technological advance.
The critique will then have a double thrust, questioning the perspectives and

priorities of those who decide the design of the technology (and its supporting infrastructures), while also heeding those who will have to cope with the consequences of how it is produced and used.

UNMASKING THE POWERS

Evaluation, therefore, involves listening on a very broad front: there are few people unaffected by the powers deriving from technology. Most crucial is the effect of these powers on the quality of relationships, between individuals, within organized human associations, with other parts of the natural world, and with God.

1. Who exercises control and who is empowered?

Dominant production technologies have 'division of labour' as a key element, with control and efficiency as major goals. The overall strategy is defined by 'directors'; control of the work is in the hands of 'managers'. The creative relationship between a person and their work is often lost: the majority of workers have no stake in the 'whole' enterprise and no latitude to make situational judgements; they are locked into someone else's economic and power objectives ... Making matters worse, as the global consumer market develops, we are discouraged from celebrating difference, as well as impoverished by a loss of diversity in many aspects of life.

...

2. What is it that really matters?

In a process of mutual reinforcement, production technology has been harnessed to the narrow criteria of economic growth and improved 'performance', as if this would create 'wealth' and 'quality of living'. But the whole approach leaves out of the count the experiences and relationships that truly give significance to people's lives, involving expressions of love, trust, compassion, respect, delight and wonder. ...

...

3. Parts or wholes?

Ideas of justice have not escaped the mentality nurtured by production technology: concentration is on the parts (individuals and their defined rights and contractual responsibilities) rather than the whole (growth of community through equitable sharing and mutual partnership). In reproduction technologies, for example, the human body is treated too readily in terms of transferable parts, subject to quality control and bargaining over rights, rather than giving prime consideration to the relationships involved. In other fields, developing technologies have opened the way to privatizing 'the commons', enabling shared benefits to be split into individually acquired profitable parts, such as the patenting of life-forms, or cutting down swathes of tropical forest for commercial gain. Technologies would not be developed to service this kind of exploitation if a different perception of justice was paramount, such as that described by a conference of indigenous people (echoing the biblical understanding of justice):

> We must now clearly understand that justice is the maintenance of the wholeness of creation. ... Our concept of justice must shift away from being that which protects possessions towards that which provides healing of relationships between human beings, between cultures, and between human beings and all of creation. (Quoted in Niles, 1989, p. 60)

4. Genuine communication?

'A person is a person because of other people' (Zulu proverb) and communication is our life-blood. But many so-called communication technologies are nothing of the sort: they lull us into passivity or encourage us to escape into a virtual reality, with no need to accommodate other people or co-operate with them. By contrast, there are communication technologies that put us in touch with real people in actual situations, helping us respond with our minds, hearts and creative skills. What makes the difference is not just the way these technologies are used, but what is made possible − or impossible − by the hidden design. Crucial values and powerful manipulation are literally built in.

5. False security?

In power struggles within the human community, the technology of arms has always bolstered a reliance on military strength to overpower or deter 'the enemy'. The more sophisticated and deadly the weapons, the more the strategy is reinforced. ... But human communities cannot be healed by technologies that have devastation and human suffering built into their design brief. We need technologies that bolster, not hinder, efforts to live together in peace, that could reflect the biblical emphasis on the transformation of relationships through accepting the gifts of repentance and forgiveness.

6. Ravaging the natural world

The power that technology puts into our hands – and hearts – has had a dis-astrous effect on the delicately balanced ecosystems of our planet as well as per-ilously depleting its finite resources ... Technologies will only be redeemed when the interactive effects (including social, moral and spiritual aspects) are considered, nature respected, and the true well-being of people given priority.

7. The myth of perpetual progress

Innovation is a characteristic of technology that can feed an inner assumption that change is always for the better, and the wisdom we inherit from the past has been superseded ... This assumption is directly challenged by a gospel that calls for long-term commitment, to God as known through the historical Jesus, to neighbours in mutual service, and to the wholeness of the created order. The parable of Jesus recommends firm foundations in lasting truth, rather than building one's house on the shifting sand of perpetual change.

SIGNIFICANT CHOICES

It is clear that 'there is a pressing need to understand our technological destiny from principles more comprehensive than its own' (Grant, 1986, p. 34); 'to erect around (technology) and over it other values and wisdoms that oblige us to see it in its correct perspective' (Elliott, 1988, p. 179). Those on the under-side of technology make the diagnosis from their own experience:

> Communities all over the world can see with their own eyes what is hap-pening; their problem is knowing what to do, how they can shed their prejudices, curb their dependence on materialism, control their con-sumption, somehow produce their own food and clothes without dam-aging or depleting the planet and learn to live in harmony with each other and other species. (Allen, 1995)

Matching 'biblical remembrance' to such a diagnosis can help open our eyes to the social contracts we are signing and in which we all collaborate, whether at the sharp end of the advance or as captive beneficiaries. The task is urgent.

Ruth Conway was a staff member of the Student Christian Movement, then a physics teacher, and is now pursuing a concern for technology education through VALIDATE (Values in Design and Technology Education), a special interest group of IDATER (International Design and Technology Education Research Conference).

Market wisdom or market mayhem?

Mostyn Davies

The truth is that Democratic Capitalism is a moral maze with good and evil in contention throughout its fabric precisely because it is a human institution.

THE NEW RIGHT

It is important to the New Right, and a sign of its libertarian influences, that the affluent should not have the moral worth of their generosity undermined by any form of compulsion. To the New Right the most odious form of charitable compulsion is, of course, taxation. Taxation acts like a brake on the wealth-generating machine and so, it is said, induces the very poverty which taxes are meant to alleviate.

This same fear of compulsion towards moral behaviour extends to suspicion of equal opportunities legislation and much employment law. Deregulation is not just a campaign to simplify business life but also to make it easier for employers to do as they deem best. Legislation is meant to curb only the worst excesses. For the rest, business and commercial interests are meant to be self-regulating within a market place which, it is held, will ultimately punish unethical behaviour.

To help the poor, or reduce unemployment, the affluent must generate more wealth by competing more successfully in the world economy. For their part, the poor must be willing to price themselves back into work. Poverty is cured by creating more wealth not by spreading it more thinly. So, for the New Right, the Welfare State is a superficially attractive but actually 'immoral' solution to meeting human need. By eroding competitive motivation and diverting resources from wealth generation it perpetuates the problems it is meant to solve. The point is to get individuals to take responsibility for their own lives, to earn what they need and to insure against misfortune and old age.

It is important to understand this moral underpinning of the New Right. It champions free market, competitive capitalism because it believes this system harnesses the avarice of fallen human nature in the service of human progress. Moreover, as Margaret Thatcher famously observed, there is no alternative; this is the only system which works, as the fall of the Soviet Union is held to demonstrate. Democratic Capitalism is the way the world is meant to work; in serving the best interests of successful individuals it serves the best interests of us all.

'LADDERS' AND 'TRICKLES'

A key icon in the New Right's moral edifice is the 'ladder of opportunity'. The state has a duty to ensure that such ladders are in place so that competitive individuals can climb to the position which is a just reward for their ability and endeavour. Life at the bottom of the ladder should be such as to encourage the unwilling to climb. Life at the top of the ladder should be such as to deter people from back-sliding. The New Right has a low view of human nature and believes individuals require both deterrents and incentives. The meaning of life is to succeed, to be independent and to improve the quality of life for oneself and one's family.

What makes all this work is the market. Billions of individual decisions are in constant interplay in the international forum. Out of this apparently random maelstrom emerges a patterning of economic events. The efficient and competitive are rewarded and the ineffectual are judged. The global market place is held to be utterly dispassionate and beyond morality; it simply *is*, amoral, self-determining, self-regulating. There may not be such a thing as 'society' in New Right thought, but the 'market' is a corporate reality whose movements relate to individual behaviours and choices as a flock of starlings wheels in the evening sky.

Modern information technology provides international markets with a similar capacity to wheel and deal together. Indeed, trading is now automated with computers programmed to buy and sell when certain trigger values of stocks and shares are reached. But, though the computers and the market mechanism itself may be value free, their programmes and human and institutional behaviours certainly are not. They are designed to accumulate and concentrate economic and political power. Capitalism is not driven by an altruistic vision of a better world but by the need to exploit this one for personal gain.

As wealth trickles down, power floods upwards. This is the mechanism which raises the key ethical questions which will concern Christians in public life. Against this concern, it is the claim of Democratic Capitalism that its government and international institutions can balance and contain the misuse of economic power. In any case, much accumulated wealth is held institutionally, within pension funds for example, not in the personal possession of the super rich, though they do exist. Transnational corporations are defended as good corporate citizens essential to the development of poorer nations; as the Third World serves transnational interests, so wealth from the richer nations trickles down into their economies. The question, of course, is how much trickles out of them and to what extent they are really assisted or merely exploited. A stream of notorious business scandals in recent years, together with atrocious business and environmental practices in developing countries, raise the question of just how benign modern capitalism really is. It can be argued, not least from the American example, that Democratic Capitalism polarizes society and contains the seeds of its own corruption within it.

GREAT GAINS ... BUT?

On the other hand, Democratic Capitalism can show enormous improvements to the quality of life, and life chances, of billions of ordinary people. Much of Adam Smith's dream of 'universal opulence' has been achieved. The choice and quality of goods and services which have been made affordable is extraordinary. Democratic Capitalism may be far from perfect but what preceded it was far from perfect. Its ultimate defence is that as a system it is learning to do better; it has the economic and technical power to improve the environment; if governments wish to produce greater equality, then so long as they do not kill the goose that lays the golden egg, it can be achieved. There is a plasticity, an organic quality about Democratic Capitalism which, rightly directed, promises the advancement of human civilization and the solving of its resource and ecological problems.

Well, maybe. The truth is that Democratic Capitalism is a moral maze with good and evil in contention throughout its fabric precisely because it is a human institution. We created it and it faithfully reflects both our avarice and our generosity, our creativity and our destructiveness. We should beware the idols we create and serve. Mammon has feet of clay. Maybe this is the best system we have created so far but it is still ethically primitive. Adam Smith imagined an invisible hand guiding events so that the pursuit of self-interest marvellously contributed to the common good. It was easier to see things that way in 1750 than to do so today when our earth seems so small, so wounded and so fragile.

OUR RESPONSE

So, what should the Christian in public life conclude? First, that Mammon should not be allowed to get above himself. He is a crude, stupid, primitive god however sophisticated he may appear. Smith is wrong. There is no invisible hand turning our selfishness and greed to the common good. It is a piece of gratuitous sophistry which one look at the armament industry, the Brazilian rain forest, or the unemployed, immediately exposes. Achieving the common good will not come so conveniently. It is not the function of the churches to 'baptize' Democratic Capitalism but to speak in the name of God for those things which more genuinely make for peace, justice and truth in the land.

Mostyn Davies is the Bishop of Peterborough's Chaplain for Industry.

Beyond Laurel and Hardy
Why we need a workable model of social democracy
John Kennedy

We need to develop a more sophisticated and human political economy than the crudities of Anglo-American welfare capitalism.

'ANOTHER FINE MESS'

Public life has always been marked by the difference between rhetoric and reality. Despite that, the current divergence between them still manages to astonish. British political discussion has long been dominated by the notion of the individual acting in a free society. Yet Britain has never been a more comprehensively collectivist and compulsory state ... And the whole process of government has become increasingly centralized, albeit in the name of market choice.

What we have here is a peculiar combination of collective institutions clumsily used to serve an individualist ideology. We have seen the formula played out in the cinema for half a century, by Laurel and Hardy. They show us the ever more outlandish consequences of an initial misconception until 'That's another fine mess you've gotten me into'.

Britain is experiencing a basic failure in political practice. Dogmatic over-reliance on the mechanisms of the market has created a vast burden of welfare casualties. Welfare systems have responded with a defence of individual rights which is understandable but also expensive, and politically unsustainable. Rights to individual welfare benefits have been racked up without asking serious questions about the constructive, collective, and co-operative development of society as a whole. Another bizarre subtext to this welfare imperialism is the growth of middle-class welfare. Transfer payments and service provision tend to help the prosperous disproportionately. It is well known how ineffectual health care and education expenditure is for poorer people. Thus our ways of helping people are very expensive, and ineffective. And yet still need is stigmatized as the calls to 'get tough on welfare' become more strident. There is a fearful symmetry here. There is the right to assert one's position in the market place, and there is the right to assert one's position in the welfare system. The market delivers insecure, low-paid employment, and generates mass casualties clamouring for decreasingly valuable welfare rights.

A DEVELOPMENTAL MODEL OF POLITICAL ECONOMY

We need to develop a more sophisticated and humane political economy than these crudities of Anglo-American welfare capitalism. David Marquand (1988) has suggested a developmental model of society, and his ideas have been used, here and elsewhere, to outline a European model of political economy. In this perspective, there are three broad institutional elements of public life: the market, politics and the enabling state. A fourth consists more of an attitude than an institution – civil society.

The concept of the market has proved deeply controversial, especially for Christians. For some, the market is simply a diverse system of information, in which what works best can be continually trusted. The market can plausibly be claimed to have been the most important means in history of bringing material improvement in the lot of poor people. For others, the market is incompatible with morality. Or, more modestly, some think competition fine in theory, but suspect that the powerful will always conspire to rig the market against the weak.

This conflict can be reconciled. Markets exist in a political context. In more recent years that context has developed into a complex interaction between competition and co-operation, stimulation and regulation. This includes what we will here call the enabling state.

Up to 40 per cent of national income is devoted to the provision of goods and services through complex systems of state distribution. Further benefits are distributed in the form of tax forgone. We learn together in social institutions. We keep one another healthy in systems of care. Business works best when its skills are sharpened by competition, but that competitive activity operates through sophisticated co-operation between variously skilled human beings. Nothing undermines that effort so much as the fear of being sacked.

There is a three-way interaction between the market, democratic politics and the enabling state. Social investment helps us to get into a fast-changing labour market and to stay healthy there. The revenues generated by the market sustain social investment. Democratic institutions police free markets, and set acceptable levels of taxation which ensure that the enabling state is maintained. In this model market success is as dependent on the enabling state as any other sector of society. Furthermore, market techniques can assist service distribution, if the whole operates within a collective value system.

. . .

CIVIL SOCIETY

The most important feature of a dynamic model such as the one outlined is renewal. Social systems acquire deeply ingrained mental habits and accumulate
layers of institutional vested interest. There needs to be a commitment from
the operators of such a system to step back and reflect on what is happening.
The actors must be able simultaneously to attend to their own present interests
and those of the future of the whole. The present must be managed; the future,
imagined.

. . .

This is the kind of society whose institutions have the moral confidence to create a more just and more broadly prosperous public life, richer in every sense.
Its slogan might be 'The management of change in pursuit of the common
good'. It depends heavily on the notion that life can be managed civilly,
though not without conflict. We do not have here the Kingdom of God, only
a human republic, but one that offers many forms of godliness.

In this kind of civil society everybody has to lay aside some vested interest.
Such interests are certainly the conventional ones of church, politics, business
and the enabling state. But there is also the nostalgia, deeply infecting
Christian political sentiment, which longs in a shallow way for a revolutionary
utopia. This kind of sentiment undermines serious commitment to a manage-
able model of political economy – it also leaves the stage to Laurel and Hardy.

John Kennedy has travelled widely in Asia and Central America. He has
worked on the East Coast of Sri Lanka and in the East End of London. He is
an ordained minister, and speaks for the Methodist Church on public issues.

Christian women in public life –
leaven for a new culture? (1)
Mary Grey

What operates . . . is a stereotyped, essentialist view of 'women's nature'.

It is beyond dispute that we live in a culture that is short on vision. That we
have nothing to offer the 'liberated', 'post-communist' countries but the lure of

Western capitalism and a feverish consumerism ought to be a matter of shame instead of pride. That the debates on Europe are conducted on purely economic terms – monetarist at that – ignoring profounder cultural issues, means that Christians are failing to seize what could be a 'kairos' moment for enfleshing our 2,000-year-old dream of the justice of the Kingdom of God in today's changing world.

What contribution could women now make to a work scene characterized by deep recession, where the crying need would seem to be the ability to discover a meaning in life despite endless vistas of unemployment? I suggest that public life and the world of paid employment has always been ambiguous for women. Until comparatively recently women – with the exceptions of royalty, and the foundresses of religious orders – have been in any case excluded from public life. The struggle for the vote, for access to education, the professions, political life, indeed for recognition as full human subjects, has been long and painful – and still carries on. Women are still worse paid, work longer hours and carry the double load of caring also for small children, elderly parents and home: numerous studies document that 'shared parenting' and equal distribution of household chores has simply not become a reality in the way that second-wave feminism hoped that it might.

Exclusion is one thing: but inclusion on patriarchal terms is less easily detectable. What operates here is a stereotyped, essentialist view of 'women's nature' which makes women 'suitable' for certain types of work in the public sphere, by analogy with what they do in the private sphere. This view – heavily influenced by Jungian psychology, though much older than Jung – assumes that 'the feminine nature' is more caring, compassionate and sympathetic, qualities which make women in great demand as secretaries and nurses. When Christian theology adds the quality of 'service' as the essential quality of ministry (obedient, humble service at that), it means that Christian ideology dictates that certain types of work are quintessentially 'women's work'. If we further add to this that women, through the poverty trap, are frequently forced into the lowest paid, humblest forms of work – like cleaning office blocks late into the night – the picture becomes grimmer. And among women themselves, it is women from ethnic minority groups, and single mothers, where the greatest hardship is experienced. Even worse is the way female sexuality is exploited in the work sphere, by the forcing of young girls into sweat shops, as well as into prostitution in many parts of the Third World. The fact that this is considered to be 'women's work' reflects the negative and despising attitudes towards women's sexuality, a negativity expressed also by holding women responsible for the 'moral fibre' of the younger generation.

Mary Grey is Professor in Contemporary Theology at Southampton University.

Learning communities
David Clark

The survival of the human species is about learning to live communally.

THE 'COMMUNAL DILEMMA'

The most profound challenge facing humankind at the turn of the millennium is as simply stated as it is awesome to address. I call it 'the communal dilemma'. It is the challenge of how groups and associations, organizations and institutions, and indeed whole societies, can retain a rich communal identity whilst respecting in positive and pro-active ways the communal identity of others.

The communal dilemma is no marginal phenomena. As Parker Palmer (1977), a Quaker scholar, puts it: 'Community means more than the comfort of souls. It means and has always meant, the survival of the species.' Our problem is that we have so debased the word 'community', squirting it on almost every collective noun in order to ensure that the latter smells sweet and user-friendly, that we have failed to recognize community's hugely destructive as well as immensely creative potential. For if community turns in on itself, if it becomes incestuous through fear or triumphalism, we end up with the Northern Irelands, Rwandas and Bosnias of this world. It is only where community is claimed as the hall-mark of inclusivity and our common humanity that its power to destroy can be transformed into its potential to create and unite.

COMMUNITY AS PASSION

But what is the nature of 'community' which makes it such a dynamic instrument of good or evil? Its true potential is certainly not recognizable when we use the concept to describe some vague kind of human collective resident in some vague kind of place – 'the community'. Nor is its potential realized when we speak of a community of interest such as a community association, a community health council or a monastic community. Even to link community to human relationships by talking of familial or ethnic communities does not really get to the heart of the matter.

For community, in its most dynamic sense, is not about loose collectives in boundaryless locations, it is not about shared interests or even human relationships as such, although all these may be expressions of it. Community at its root is about human passions with all their immense possibilities for good or ill.

...

Community interpreted in this way is at last a concept big enough to throw light on the challenge we face in the next millennium – 'the survival of the species'. But what are these feelings and sentiments which carry so much potential for creativity or destruction?

FEELINGS, VALUES AND BELIEFS

I argue elsewhere (Clark, 1996a) that community as feeling has three fundamental foundations – a sense of security, a sense of significance and a sense of solidarity (the Three Ss). The first is about us having a place to stand – where we feel physically safe and enjoy a state of 'well-being'. The second is about us having a part to play within whatever collective we find ourselves; that which brings us recognition and fulfilment. The third, a sense of solidarity, is about our having a world to which to belong, a group which is 'ours'; with a membership we describe as 'us'. All Three Ss matter but most important of all is the last.

These Three Ss I see as intimately related to Three Ls – the values of life, liberty and love. It is here that beliefs – in my case as a Christian – come fully into the picture. For me the two paradigms of community are the Trinity and the Kingdom of God. The doctrine of the Trinity underpins two key aspects of community. First, that the sense of being a part (significance) and of being a whole (solidarity) are the essence of what community is all about. 'One in Three and Three in One.' Second, that the three Persons of the Trinity possess attributes closely linked to my Three Ls – God as Creator (life), Christ as Liberator (liberty) and the Holy Spirit as Unifier (love).

The Kingdom of God exemplifies for me the fact that true community is inclusive not exclusive. For the Three Ss to exist within a collective determined to be an island – be that related to race, gender, wealth, faith, political ideology or whatever – is to espouse community as a nihilistic phenomenon. But if communities are seeking to become more open, more receptive and more generous to one another then we really are in the business of transformative love, divine as well as human.

To transform closed communities into open ones – to address the communal dilemma – is a massive undertaking. If we are to succeed, despite the appalling record of humankind, and succeed we must if our shrinking planet is to have a future, then one other factor has to be brought into the equation – that of learning.

EDUCATION

'The survival of the (human) species' depends on learning to live communally. This is a process that depends on a very different understanding of education from that which at present permeates our education system. Education at its richest is not about nurture, instruction or training, let alone indoctrination. It is about learning to learn. It is a life-focused and person-centred process of discovery engaged in with other partners in learning. It is about questioning values and beliefs not in an iconoclastic way, but as expressing an openness to truth – in oneself, in others and in the cosmos.

Community needs genuine education because without it inclusivity can easily turn to exclusivity, the journey out can give way to fear of freedom and become the journey in again. Community needs education because community building is an art which has to be learnt the hard way – there can be no quick fixes from above or below. Community needs true learning to sustain it over the many generations that will be required to turn our world into a community of open communities.

But education also needs community. Any collective – be it family, school, church, hospital, business or government itself – which neglects its communal health will hugely weaken the ability to educate. Without a sense of security, of significance and of solidarity, learning soon falters and loses its zest and zeal. This is why it is imperative that all those institutions which assume responsibility for the education of society become learning communities within which community enriches education, and education frees community for a universalizing role.

A LEARNING WORLD

There is of course more to the creation of a learning world, made up of learning societies and learning communities, than this. There are massive forces of exclusivity and closure to be overcome. It is here that faith so often comes to the fore – for me in a God who forgives, redeems and empowers, often at immense cost. It is here that life, liberty and love become not just academic concepts but words that have to be made flesh in the mess and mire of everyday living. But, in the end, the call remains and demands a response – to work for the Kingdom Community to come on earth as in heaven.

All this demonstrates just how vital are our communities of learning – family, church, school, university ... They do not exist simply to pass on the culture, to enhance individual fulfilment or to equip people to fit into the production process. They exist to be microcosms of society as a true learning community so that as we grow up and grow away we know how to become citizens of not only this or that country, but of a whole world which now has to be our future. The medium of our learning has to be the message if we are to turn the power of community from one which can enslave and destroy, into one which frees and unifies humankind.

Responding to a culture in crisis
John Austin

The bonds keeping together the fabric of our common life are ... in danger of unravelling.

The institutions of any society carry the values and aspirations of their society. They are the means by which the attitudes and values of a society, or a group of people within it, are conveyed from one generation to the next. Institutions, particularly those espoused by the powerful in a society, become major expressions of the culture of which they are part. One has but to reflect on the significance for our culture of such institutions as the Monarchy, the Law, the Unions, the Civil Service, the NHS, to see that they still remain, though to a diminishing extent, expressions of shared values and commonly understood ways of doing things. They are even now significant expressions of the culture that influences us all.

THE CRISIS OF OUR INSTITUTIONS

However, when you look at the institutions of our country at the moment there is no doubting that almost every single one of them is in real crisis. They are afflicted by a crisis of morale; or a crisis of direction; or a crisis of purpose; or a crisis of corruption; or a crisis of legitimacy. They are afflicted by one or more of these crises and are less and less able to be the value bearers or to shape commonly understood ways by which individuals and groups relate to one another in society.

If you look at the centres of financial power, or the police, or even the legal profession itself, corruption has corroded their authority. Or if you look at the teaching or medical or social work professions or those involved in public service, there is a huge loss of morale and sense of purpose. Or if you examine the political system itself, there is a grave loss of legitimacy ... Or if you look at the family, it is clearly failing to be the means of affirmation, security and love for an enormous number of people. I can think of no institution in our society which has escaped the institutional crisis of our day.

An institutional crisis of this dimension is, however, indicative of a culture which is itself in major crisis. The bonds keeping together the fabric of our common life are clearly in danger of unravelling.

THE CRISIS OF VALUES

Behind the separate crisis of our institutions lies a crisis of value. The values enshrined within our institutions no longer guide those involved in our institutions in the way they once did. How many Christians who committed themselves to the police, to teaching, to local government, to the law or medicine or to social work, as an act of service, out of a sense of vocation, now find themselves working in an environment deeply alien to the one they experienced when they made their original commitment? Much of their alienation stems from the decay of values or betrayal of values they believed in and understood their institution or profession to embody. Values of truth, of care, of trust, of dignity, of integrity, of honesty, of generosity, of self-sacrifice, no longer seem to guide the behaviour and direction of our institutions.

So perhaps one of our tasks in this Decade of Evangelization is to help groups of Christians and others articulate and identify the values that are under threat in the institutions in which they work and to develop strategies through which these values can be strengthened and given clearer expression.

...

THE CRISIS OF BELIEF

However, we betray the Gospel if we concern ourselves only with values. We need to see that if values are not nurtured in the soil of faith then, like cut flowers, they bloom for a season but in the end wither. The decay of values is intimately related to loss of faith. Values are about being accountable to a transcendent reality, conformity to whose will and purpose offers the only way to human wholeness and well-being. It is the discovery of this truth that sets us free. It is from the vantage point of belief in the will and purposes of God for humankind and for the whole of creation revealed in Jesus Christ, that we need to make our affirmations of what is good in institutions and the common life of our society and pronounce our anathemas against the prevailing idolatries of our age.

So another task in the process of evangelization of our culture is to reintroduce belief into our discussion of values. We need to point out the vulnerability of values that are not nurtured by belief.

'THE CULTURE OF CONTENTMENT'

One of the prevailing idolatries which we need to confront in the Decade of Evangelization is what John Kenneth Galbraith, the American social and economic commentator, calls 'the culture of contentment', itself the almost inevitable outcome of the self-serving individualism which has confined the discussion of social purpose and direction to the realm of personal morality and individual opinion. He describes 'the culture of contentment' which afflicts us as having four fundamental characteristics:

1. Those who benefit from it are receiving their just deserts.
2. Short-term public inaction is always preferred to long-term action no matter what the consequences. There is a refusal to pay now for what will benefit future generations.
3. A highly subjective view is taken of the State or of government. It is approved of when it intervenes to protect the interests of those benefiting from the *status quo* but not when its intervention is needed to protect the vulnerable.
4. The contented show great tolerance of enormous differentials in income.
5. There is a fifth characteristic not mentioned by Galbraith but one which is a powerful characteristic of the culture. The contented have a cavalier attitude to the truth. It can be massaged, packaged, distorted by being used economically; it is not something to take responsibility for or to resign over.

Such a culture is profoundly Godless and on every count runs contrary to a culture impregnated with the meanings and purposes, the possibilities and invitation to human beings revealed by God in Jesus Christ. The bankrupt nature of our social vision is nowhere more apparent than in the number of homeless people. It is clearly a moral outrage when the public sector borrowing requirement is deemed more important than homes for the citizens of this still wealthy land. But it is not simply a failure of moral vision. It is symptomatic of a failure of belief. We will not restore the bonds of our common life nor a sense of our common humanity until we have recovered our awareness of and our belief in the transcendent Reality and discovered there Grace and Truth.

. . .

John Austin is Bishop of Aston.

A new kind of faith

Faith is a gift. But it is also a living experience and nurtures a growing understanding of God at work in today's world which by its very nature has to be communicated and shared. Faith is about eternal truths; but it is also about meaning and purpose for each generation in its own particular historical and cultural context. If faith is not renewed and reinterpreted for each generation, it is reduced to dogmatism or banality.

In response to the fundamental issues raised in the previous section, the writers below present a number of themes which appear to be energizing and shaping the response of faith for our time.

One theme is around 'The Trinity of Love, one God in Perfect Community' as the Iona Community's *Worship Book* puts it (1991, p. 17). Two affirmations have to be made by Christians in this context: first that people are of infinite value in the eyes of God and thus irreplaceable. Secondly, that personal growth as well as corporate fulfilment depend on the quality of relationships which characterize human affairs. A true spirituality for today's world is rooted in an awareness of our profound cosmic interconnectedness.

Another theme relates to the nature of the Kingdom of God, which reveals not only the way things ought to be, but the way things have to be if human civilization is to survive very far into the next millennium. This means a re-affirmation of those values which give pride of place to the marginalized, and the breaking down of those divides which isolate and alienate one person or group from other.

All this presupposes that the Gospel is not confined to a private or sacred arena but is seen as the heart of the matter, bearing witness to divine love as the cosmic reality which, if ignored or rejected, will mean the ultimate collapse of all our social and political endeavours.

Reflections of a Christian humanist

Helen Oppenheimer

A person can be defined as an irreplaceable centre of mattering.

'People matter' is a platitude which deserves attention (see Oppenheimer, 1983; 1995). Both unbelievers and believers are apt to behave as if they had forgotten it. Some seem not to care about other people. Others say they care but talk about God's Will in a way that belittles God's children. I call myself a 'Christian humanist'. 'Humanist' means several things, and has been hijacked to mean somebody who believes in human beings without God. Is it too late for 'humanist' to mean someone who affirms, and builds upon, the platitude that human beings matter? People are not all that matters, but they are the clearest example of mattering.

Christian humanists believe people matter to God. God the Creator is the great Humanist, who valued people enough to enter human life and die a human death. Humanists who have no God need not talk a different language about people. There is room for a large overlap in understanding. Believers and unbelievers need not be afraid of working together with a shared vision of human value. 'Vision' and 'value' are strong words, but vague words. It is easier to talk about the value of people than to be precise about what this means. What are people to be valued for? If we value attractive, intelligent, loving people, do ugly, stupid, badly-behaved people not matter, or not matter as much? But if we value them whatever they are like, just because they are people, then do good qualities count for nothing?

'Good looks don't matter. Brains don't matter. The real person lies deeper.' How much deeper? Virtue too may depend on luck: upbringing, circumstances or disposition. Is the 'real person' the remainder when everything interesting is removed? 'The soul' is more like an onion than a nut: layers of reality, not a hard expendable shell hiding the valuable kernel. If we put aside the theories about what should matter, we find what does matter is the whole pattern of this person. When we value people we value them as wholes. We know this, but how can we apply it?

THE VALUE OF PEOPLE

Many troubles are caused by people not being valued enough. Is there any recipe for making the world a better place? If that looks like a leading question, calling for obvious answers, traditional, liberal or radical, the point is made.

One recipe for *not* making the world a better place is predicting what line someone will take, slotting people into categories. Small annoyances and huge tragedies grow from the tendency of human beings to stereotype one another and themselves. Here are some examples:

At her age she must be out of touch.
I haven't time.
He is unemployable.
That child is ineducable.
How like a man!
Vegetarians are cranky.
Blacks are savages.
Whites are racists.
The children won't notice.
She is poor but honest.
She's a woman so she must be
  gentle and home-loving.
He is rich and grasping.
You wouldn't understand.

Young people are so inconsiderate.
Scientists are cold-hearted.
He won't join in so he must be
  snobbish.
She talks a lot so she must be
  conceited.
I'm too old to learn new ways.
Single mothers are feckless: or
  heroines.
Foreigners are comic.
He's a delinquent: he must have
  unloving parents.
Men don't cry.

One can enjoy making a list like this: the more annoying, the more enjoyable: but it is serious. The examples are mixed but the attitude they represent is one attitude. Many well-meaning people are trapped within it unawares. Many more are hurt by it. Misery can start here. At the least, our pleasure in one another's company is spoilt. Prejudice is like smoking: never starting is easier than giving up.

How can we realize that everyone matters? The Christian answer, 'Love one another', rewords the problem: 'Yes, but how?'

Christians have a clue which they underestimate: they are told to love others as themselves. Must they go one better ('No, more than ourselves')? People are so used to assuming that Christianity is all about unselfishness that self-love seems embarrassing; but there is nothing loving about saying 'I'm useless'. Who wants me to look on myself as a poor worm? If people matter to me, I cannot opt out of mattering to them. It dishonours God to think of God's creatures as no good.

Like it or not, we have to begin with self-love. The teaching of Christ is more realistic than some Christians imagine. We are not required to perform moral contortions, but to see all human beings in this one light. My own self is neither more nor less special. I know at first hand the infinite value of one person. Self-love is a sample exercise shown to us, a beginning not an end. The valuing and loving that make life worthwhile can develop in all directions.

I AND WE

We start with ourselves; but not with ourselves alone, as if it were a mystery how we found other people. Babies learn 'I' and 'We' together by having wants and being cherished. Everyone is the centre of a world; and all these worlds are interlocked. My mattering could never be all the mattering there is. Loving is discovering one another's mattering.

Saying 'Down with self: up with others' is useless, and needless. This 'down' and 'up' cannot be distinct. Giving and taking are two sides of one coin. 'Give and take' is supposed to be a commonsense recipe for not falling to blows. You want to take and you do some giving for the sake of peace. Say rather: giving and taking are what make life worth living, and at the best we hardly know which is which. Selfishness is not a forbidden treat but a sort of solitary confinement. To turn in on oneself is hell. If anyone says 'Why bother about love?' the answer is that calling love compulsory is like calling food compulsory: we starve without it.

IRREPLACEABILITY

A person can be defined as an irreplaceable centre of mattering. The value of a person is that another one will not do. I know nobody else is a substitute for me: and everyone is a Me. To say that each one is special is better than to say, more boringly, that they are all equal. To look at people in the light of their ir-replaceability is to see what their value means.

This tiresome person has a point of view. It may be easier to consider that this person had a mother. Nobody is a substitute for somebody's child. Christians can go on to say, still talking the same language about people, that nobody is a substitute for God's child. The love commandment seems less impossible. To benefit from this line of thought we must keep it concrete. What matters is not the abstract idea of a person but this particular person, valuable neither as identical nor as better but as unique.

LIKING

Well-meaning people say: We have to love but we do not have to like. Liking doesn't matter. We find some people congenial and there it is, but loving is willing people's good. Are we convinced? How do we feel about someone whose evident dislike is wrapped in talk of Christian love? No wonder 'charity' has shrunk its meaning. 'I don't want charity' means 'I don't want good done to me out of duty'. Human beings often need help, but they want to be liked.

In fact we have more control over our likings than our loving. Virtuous ef-fort collapses into meanness and crossness, whereas people who attend to one another with a readiness to be pleased have made a start. Liking is an approach to loving. There is more to almost anybody than first appears. If the stereotyping could stop, we could realize that other people are as special as we feel ourselves to be.

Liking, of course, cannot be the whole answer. Huge problems about sin and hate, forgiveness and reconciliation remain. Yet sin is often failure to attend. The work of a prophet, an artist, a mediator, or even a fund-raiser is to invite people's attention. Looking lays foundations for liking. People who attend do not need so much forgiving and reconciling.

Helen Oppenheimer is a graduate of Lady Margaret Hall, Oxford, and writes on Christian ethics and philosophical theology. She has served on various Church of England commissions, mainly on marriage and divorce, and received a Lambeth Doctorate of Divinity in 1993.

Spirituality on the super-highway
Peter Challen and colleagues

(A freely plagiarizing reflection – the outcome of discussions between friends who plod their by-way beside the 'super-highway')

There is a temptation to relegate spirituality to private practice. It belongs to public life ... Spirituality is the focusing of human awareness on the subtle aspects of existence, a practice that reveals to us profound interconnectedness.

There is a temptation to relegate spirituality to private practice. It belongs to public life ... Spirituality is the focusing of human awareness on the subtle aspects of existence, a practice that reveals to us profound interconnectedness. It is to receive into our frail piece of mortal flesh an awareness of the whole system within ourself. If we reach towards that, even our death would be a celebration of life. Spirituality is a human development that transports into a fragile but living vessel an image of the beauty, delicacy and purpose of the entire universe, with a consciousness of the loving energy that created it.

To discover this kind of spirituality we must pass from a notion of religion that is sectarian, parochial in the narrow sense, territorial and static, introverted and imported, to a notion that is catholic and evangelical, authentic and interior, dynamic and adult. It will portray the Jewish ideal, 'that spirituality is to be normal in the night of darkness and in times of constant insecurity'.

Spirituality is the innocent completeness of our material reality. It is the mysterious universe beyond our shallow perceptions of what is real. It is the state of humble wonder and fresh commitment to daily life, in which we are encouraged by energizing memories and summoned by hope.

There is a profound simplicity about spirituality. Mystery is not the unintelligible, but the inexhaustibly intelligible. Since we should have no illusion that we will get out of this world alive, let us build into our mind a coherence about the most profound questions of human destiny, so that our spiritual part can tolerate with ease the loss of the mortal part. A condition of that state is to know that vulnerability is a precondition of open, maturing, lively, life-transcending faith. This was well put by one of those in this dialogue: 'There are no solutions, only ways of living that enable us to cradle new life, while surviving old death.'

Another condition of spirituality in a material world is to know and put into practice the insistent paradox that life is a coherent diversity. Such coherent diversity comprises 'an integrated code' (the coherence of all interests for the common good) in an ever more creative and dynamic tension with many 'collected codes' (each discipline rightly pursuing its own professional contribution) pertinent to specific tasks and norms.

. . .

A very short sentence has served me well of late in the gentle task of evoking explorations into God; that is, the task of perceiving the practicalities of faith effectively informing ordinary work. It echoes words by a theologian, Moberly, that 'Spirit is the meaning of matter and matter is the method of spirit'. My triggering abbreviation is 'spirit is matter seen in a stronger light'. Claire, Colin, Sabine, Simon, Rosemary, Rupert, Pamela, Oonagh, Garth, Steb, Barrie and Neal are a few of those who have been sparked into new enthusiasms by that sentence, opening me up to their own notable searchings and discoveries around the theme. Thus they have reminded me that we should not fail to make some links between the vast new global network possible on the 'information highway' and the spiritual requirement of a sense of the awesome integrated mystery of which we are a part. The sadness is that the tyranny of our professional disciplines so often retains no serious brief for the whole.

Along the highway 'connectivity' is one of the 'in' words for information technology buffs, just as 'creation' and 'body of Christ' are for Christian enthusiasts, and 'holism' is for eco-freaks. As ideas cross frontiers we find extraordinary resonance between the varying and dynamic languages with which we all exercise our curiosity about meaning and purpose. Which takes me to another sentence that has served me well: 'a work of art is hard work that crosses forbidding boundaries and opens up things unseen, forgotten or even undreamt'. Such a human 'work of art' is the one who would be spiritual while still engrossed in and responsible for the material world, where our response-ability is to be exercised, for a span at least.

Even as I say this, we must be quick to recognize that without the frequent rehearsal of true spirituality in the various ways suggested ... the development of a vast information network may well not be the road to a just and peaceable global village, but towards a negatively chaotic reflection of a global middle-class suburb. While the immense possibilities of new connectivity open up around us there is an ever-present danger of a vast new impoverishment; that of the millions who have no access to the 'super-highway'.

Hold the vision: live in response-ability ... of 'spirit as matter seen in stronger light', even at your computer terminal, your desk, on your mobile phone, or at your bench, as you invent diverse subordinate text designs for contributing to the greater contextual ecological coherence of life itself.

Peter Challen was until recently Senior Chaplain of the South London Industrial Mission and Rector of the inner-city parish that gives SLIM its focus. He is a Sloan Fellow of the London Business School and a Fellow of the RSA, where he participated in the 'Tomorrow's Company' inquiry in the work group on the 'Company as a living system'. He was recently made a Freeman of Southwark, in recognition of ministry that serves the whole community.

The power of the Kingdom
The message of Christians in public life
David Clark

At the heart of the cosmos is not a massive chemical reaction, unbounded energy, or even a ritu-alistic mystery but Persons in relationship.

...

'THE WAY THINGS ARE'

The message of the Kingdom addresses head-on the two major challenges of our day – the crisis of life or death, and of meaning or despair. The former is a search for enduring forms of community in a global context, the latter the quest for a truth which can give point and purpose to living. Both journeys are an integral part of the quest for the Kingdom.

The Kingdom reveals the truth about 'the way things are': all else is, at best, lay-by or cul-de-sac. Unless we take seriously – as seriously as life and death – that which the Kingdom demonstrates about 'the way things are', we shall end up in an unholy mess. Community, that which the Kingdom portrays as an essential outworking of truth, will continue to be a chimera, and chaos, not the King, will reign.

But what is 'the way things are' of which we need to take note if the crises of life or death and of meaning or despair are to bring opportunity and not destruction? What is the nature of this 'Truth' to which Christians in public life are called to bear witness as they travel through a pluralistic and bewildering world?

THE TRUTH IS PERSONAL

The Kingdom points to a King. Its message is that reality, and Truth, are profoundly personal. At the heart of the cosmos is not a massive chemical reaction, unbounded energy, or even a ritualistic mystery – but Persons in relationship. And if that is true for the cosmos, it is true also for our minuscule and momentary part of it. 'The way things are' is that life and existence are founded on persons in relationship. Unless in our public life this is acknowledged as the ultimate norm for all analyses, evaluation, judgements and decisions, nothing will work.

The interpersonal nature of ultimate reality expressed through the image of the Kingdom means that it is relationships, divine and human, which are the ground of our being. But the Kingdom declares more. For it signals that these relationships are energized and empowered by 'an exchange of love', as Rosemary Haughton (1981) puts it. It is a passionate love, which takes each and every person to be of unique value, and a continuous giving and receiving of such love on which all community, divine and human, ultimately rests.

If Persons (and persons) in relationship demonstrate 'the way things are', then all attempts to put that which is impersonal, however conceptually clever or noble, at the centre of life are courting disaster. Christians in public life here face an onslaught on the meaning of life to which they are, at all costs, called to bear witness. For no philosophy, ideology or creed *per se* can replace the centrality of loving relationships without 'good' becoming evil. There is, for example, no more possibility of salvation for the Eastern bloc in an impersonal capitalism than there was in an impersonal communism. Indeed there is no future for any society which puts its faith in the ideology of an inhuman market – in which people become primarily the means to serve the process of wealth creation. The Kingdom – 'the way things are' and the only way things can work – is not about value for money but about the value of people. If Christians have a model to offer it is not that of the market, but that of the meal to which all are invited irrespective of economic worth because the King wants them there.

Nor can we substitute nationalism or ethnicity for personhood. Though seeming to be about the personal, these are, at best, forms of relationship which can often deny the universality of community and, at worst, inhuman and destructive ideologies.

. . .

Not even a call to return to altruistic 'values', however worthy, can replace the personal foundations of the Truth to which Christians in public life bear witness. Christians do not worship 'the good', or even 'the common good', but a God of love, engaged in a living and affirming exchange of love with all his people.

THE TRUTH IS COMMUNAL

Because the Truth is about Persons (and persons) in relationship, it is intensely communal. The search for the Kingdom is thus a search for a Kingdom Community. The Christian picture of such a Community is the Trinity, in which the uniqueness of each Person is affirmed within the intimate unity of the whole. The Trinity points to a Kingdom Community not as product but as process, a never-ending exchange of life and love between Persons of infinite value.

This interpersonal process of being, belonging and becoming is as vital for human as for divine community. We seek human dignity embraced by human solidarity. But in the context of public life, a myriad powers, great and small, block that search. Love is not exchanged. Life and meaning are threatened by death and despair. Boundaries – of race, class, gender, age – become insuperable divides. The arduous search for identity and belonging sends us scurrying into the ghetto or wandering in the wilderness.

Christians in public life declare, in deed as often as word, that the search for the Kingdom Community is about crossing these divides. Because this is the only way things will work, no human institution, from the family to the nation, no school, no hospital, no factory, no commercial enterprise, no multinational company – and no church – can live and grow if it is closed in on itself. The Berlin Wall is a symbol which must not be forgotten. Whatever the 'product' sought, be it justice or peace, children educated or washing powder, patients cured or fork-lift trucks repaired, if we perpetuate rather than overcome that which blocks the exchange of love, we will self-destruct.

The Kingdom Community is about openness not closure, collaboration before competition. In exchanges, individual or international, working for the Kingdom is about honouring the contribution of others, about listening and learning and living together. It is a risky process just because so much of public life is founded on the impersonal, on self-protection, on mistrust and on manipulation. Thus Christians in public life are always vulnerable to ridicule, exploitation and abuse. But their resources are unequalled – for the power, of the interpersonal, as well as the glory, is God's.

THE TRUTH IS POWERFUL

The power of Persons (and, therefore, persons) in relationship is infinite. It is that power which gave birth to cosmos and crocus alike. It is the power of love exchanged and life continuously created. Yet it is totally uncoercive – and thus often hidden from our view, like the mustard seed in the soil and the yeast in the dough. It is the power that enables nature to bear fruit, people to bear children and civilizations to thrive and grow. It is the power of forgiveness, of reconciliation, of healing, of hope, of joy and of laughter.

The power of the Kingdom often seems weak, even foolish. Because it is so vulnerable, so often blocked and negated, it appears irrelevant, naïve, 'romantic' to 'the powers that be'. Yet the power of the Truth, of the genuinely personal and interpersonal, of true community, cannot be held back. Like the underground spring it eventually breaks through – sometimes gently, sometimes violently. Christians in public life bear witness not to a fatalistic and divisive philosophy of *laissez-faire*, but to the confrontation of the impersonal with the interpersonal, the inhuman with the human, the death-dealing with the life-giving.

To be a Christian in public life is to be profoundly political, for the political is about power. It is to be ever testing 'the spirits' to see if their power is that of love exchanged or of love denied. Be it in commerce or education, welfare or healing, law and order or leisure, the ultimate norm for the Christian is that of the power of Persons, and thus persons, in relationship, of people valued whoever they are, of an open exchange of love which gives life and meaning to the whole of humanity. Christians in public life are in the business of power – the power of the Trinity and the power of the Kingdom – or they are not in business at all.

Gardens and cities

Rowan Williams

A society where there is no scope for the 'creative' is an offence to the God of Scripture.

One of the old chestnuts often repeated about the Bible narrative is that it begins in a garden and ends in a city; and this in fact offers quite a fruitful starting point for thinking about the biblical picture of human beings. The progress from gardener to citizen charts an important route in the growth of what it might mean to be human, a route that we could understand, perhaps, as a development in how we look at our environment. At the beginning, the human agenda looks deceptively simple: there is a material environment that requires 'cultivating'. The given world around is first and foremost experienced as a world of natural processes, which need to be worked with so as to maximize the benefit to human beings. But as time goes on, the environment shifts; we become aware that we not only have to struggle with and make sense of natural processes: we also have to struggle with and make sense of other selves, other wills, that are also trying to make sense of a material environment.

Now I do not for a moment imagine that this is a strict and factual account of how human beings ever really thought – as if there were a time when a human individual only ever had to worry about the 'natural' environment, and did not have to bother with other humans, other subjects. But to put it in this way does tell us something about aspects of our growth as persons. The more we grow, the more aware we become of the solidity of other people and their projects; and the less we shall be inclined to treat other subjects as if they were objects. Indeed, the more we move along this trajectory, the less we shall be inclined to treat the material environment itself as if it were just passive stuff lying around, and the more we shall learn to attend to and respect its structures and rhythms. Being a gardener is about drawing out of the material environment some shape or some outcome that is not just casual but represents something about the gardener's human mind and imagination. The good garden is marked by co-operation between that mind and imagination and the given processes of nature. And in this respect, of course, the gardener is no different from any other kind of artist.

But being a citizen is a lot more complex. Here something has to be drawn out that is not just the result of an individual imagination working with impersonal processes; being a 'good citizen' (not an easy concept to define these days) has to do with working for a shape or outcome that represents the working together of several wills, several minds. It is something that needs language for its advancement, and that never reaches a point of immobility – because the words used and the processes gone through are always generating new questions, or revealing that what has just been said or thought represents an imperfect, a faulty resolution.

Gardener and citizen alike are being involved *actively* with their environment. That, surely, is one of the basic elements in the biblical picture of humanity: the story of the Hebrew Bible begins with a human being receiving instructions to tend or cultivate the soil; and goes on to speak about a community that is called by God to work unceasingly at the details of their common life in order to make known in the world the character of the God who calls – a community that lives under 'law', the ordinances given by God, in order to make the life of the people transparent to the divine character. It is interesting to see how often the rationale of statements in the books of law in the Old Testament is said to be that they reveal something about the character of God – holiness, faithfulness, compassion for the powerless.

CREATIVITY

It is not, I think, going too far to say that the biblical picture assumes that human beings have a creative relation to their environment, and in this respect mirror the nature of God. And it follows too that certain forms of human life are deeply at odds with what the Bible sketches as the heart of being human. A society where there is no scope for the 'creative' is an offence to the God of Scripture. This is not just a comment confined to the arts. It is about the ways in which a society does or does not make space for persons to exercise a relation to the environment that is active and transformative. Take away certain civil liberties or rights of association, and the role of the human being as citizen evaporates; but there may still be room for the gardener – whether it is the long-term prisoner taming birds, the unemployed worker in the North-East growing prize leeks or the playwright in the old Soviet bloc producing subversive comedies.

It is worth noting, however, that there can be a preoccupation with 'civil liberties' that has the effect of stifling the gardening impulse – as in societies where, though basic political rights of some sort are guaranteed, the untrammelled 'rights' of free enterprise produce a market-obsessed culture in which the primary form of 'transformative activity' is selling people things and where, in consequence, small-scale and non-profitable engagements with the environment are squeezed out.

STRIKING A BALANCE

In theological discussion over the last couple of decades, the pendulum has been swinging wildly. There was a powerful fashion for a while of according to the city a kind of privileged status. Urban life represented a decisive triumph over the non-human environment, and growing technical resources could mop up the remaining social difficulties. This shows, in retrospect, a staggering naïvety about how power is exercised in urban settings and a blithe indifference to the actual forces that make for urbanization in a culture (though this could have been learned in Africa or Latin America or the Far East in the 1960s and 70s). Thus there is now a growing revolt against the urban, a nostalgia for the garden, or even for something more basic than the garden: so-called 'deep' ecological theory looks for a relation to the non-human environment that is hardly going to transform anything, conveniently bracketing some uncomfortable questions both about the means of production in the foreseeable future and about the control of disease.

It is undoubtedly hard work to find a balance here, but it is work worth doing. If these reflections about transforming involvement as the basis alike of gardening and citizenship are anywhere near truth, we have at least a critical tool for asking how specific urban and other environments work. There is no such thing as 'The City': there are urban agglomerates (i.e. social units characterized by the localizing or centralizing of commercial activities, the differentiation of work and home environments, the provision of facilities for several sub-communities on a centralized basis, and so on). They are successful in varying degrees in evoking or fostering a sense of being actively engaged in the management of an environment, involved in the processes of negotiating with other subjects, alien wills, in the definition of a good that is recognizable by more than one interest group. And where urban existence is increasingly desolate or powerless, there is a massively important job to be done in identifying quite simply where the areas are in which a difference can be made, and how resistance to a crippling imbalance of power and interest can be made more possible.

A mural on the walls; a credit union; a programme of action to keep a facility open; a secondhand clothes shop; a childcare rota; a well-attended party meeting; a locally run youth club; and, yes, a church, when it is doing its job – all these lie somewhere on the spectrum between gardening and citizenship because all witness to the residual but obstinate possibilities of transforming action, active engagement. For the Christian, they are also to do with the uncovering of the divine image – not only the image of God as creative but also the image of the Christ whose new creation is built on the faithful presence of God within humanly hopeless situations. From the point of view of theology, a self-aware and critical urban politics is a natural outgrowth of what Christians think people are for; and the experience of such a politics can in turn breathe new life into the concepts of theology. This is a conversation that has to be laboured at more and more.

Rowan Williams is Bishop of Monmouth.

Christian women in public life – leaven for a new culture? (2)

Mary Grey

Feminist theology offers ... a transformative vision of culture and public life.

Drawing not merely on the biblical and Christological image of 'the discipleship of equals' (Schüssler-Fiorenza's phrase; 1992) feminist theology offers a transformative vision of culture and public life. I draw together the resources which spell this out:

1. The agenda of 'equal rights' for women in public life is shown to be a necessary but incomplete step on the way to the transformation of culture. Simply to be included is not the goal: inclusion on whose terms is the question.
2. The biblical inspiration of being created in *imago Dei* (Gen 1 – 2) is reclaimed, not only as meaning that both sexes are called to embody the divine (in rejection of any 'complementary' theory – 'equal but different') – but in the sense that the fundamental meaning of divine creation is both relational and organic. God yearned for relationship, to share the good earth, wrote Carter Heyward (1984), but centuries of anthropocentric thinking have served to legitimize the plundering of earth's resources. Mutuality-in-relating is a cherished paradigm in feminist theology – and the relating concerned articulates the challenge to ecological justice.
3. Feminist ethics strives to create different frameworks for the ethics of public life other than the logic of domination and control. Carol Gilligan (1982) called for an 'Ethics of care and responsibility'; Sharon Welch (1990) described a 'Feminist ethic of risk' which could challenge the unjust power relations which structure our world. Repeatedly, the feminist ethicists challenge us to 'make the connections' between the ongoing oppressions which afflict the public arena. Feminist theology is thus an agenda which transcends simply 'justice for women': it is rather an ongoing transformative process, uncovering the links between sexism, racism, classism, militarism, ecocidal policies, ageism and so on ... At the same time another tune is being danced to, another tapestry is being weaved ...
4. Feminist theology reclaims the Jesus story as the story of 'bringing the margins to the centre'. As in the time of Jesus, so in our own culture, women, black people and cultural minorities, the gay communities, children and the elderly, the unemployed and homeless and the needs of the

environment, are systemically marginalized: thus a feminist liberation theology of culture makes the well-being of these groups its focus – not in
order to create a new centre (matriarchy instead of patriarchy), but to
transform our cultural matrix.

5.   The Christology which inspires this, I call a 'Christology of Connection'
(Grey, 1989), a relational, ecological, political Christology. This re-images
Christ not only as empowering women, children and ethnic minorities
into the fullness of being, but as himself being empowered by the encounter. Jesus gave embodiment to the vulnerability of God, a God who
shares the fragility and ambiguity of life on earth. This is not to build a
new mystique into powerlessness and vulnerability: there is no particular
glory in being powerless and vulnerable. What we try to do is to crack
open the myth on which public life is built, the defences built by the rich
and powerful to avoid both their own fear of death, sickness and mortality,
and the threat of 'natural' disaster, defences which set up a structural blind-
ness and a deafness with regard to all those caught in the trap of poverty
and homelessness.

But far from implying that the role of women in public life is confined to
social work with the marginalized, crucial as this certainly is, I argue that the
task is to 'make the connections' in whatever form of public involvement in
which we are situated. Access will always be a primary, fundamental task – and
access on whose terms, is the issue. But having gained access, how will the territory be transformed? What are the decision-making processes, the power relations in operation? What is the agenda being addressed by the institution?
Whose interests are being served? What are the values which govern the daily
interaction between employees? How can the breakthrough be effected from a
pure profit-oriented motivation, to a venture which takes seriously environmental issues, ecological justice and political justice for the southern hemi-
sphere?

The task is a crucial challenge to Christian educators. Unless the prophetic
material from the Bible and tradition is made accessible as resources for the
struggle, Christianity is dismissed as an archaic irrelevance for social transformation. Feminist liberation theology attempts to reclaim buried treasure to
enflesh the dream of Shalom.

The Gospel as public truth

Lesslie Newbigin

To affirm the gospel as public truth is to invite acceptance of a new starting point for thought, the truth of which will be proved only in the course of a life of reflection and action which proves itself more adequate to the totality of human experience than its rivals.

The Gospel is an account of things which have happened. It is not a proposition in metaphysics or a programme for ethics and politics, though it has implications in both these spheres. It is narrated history, and (like all narrated history) it is told with a belief about its meaning. This belief is that the story tells what God has done for the redemption of all creation and its reconciliation to the source of all being.

The story is made available to us through the living memory of the church, the community which from its beginning has been enabled by the work of the Holy Spirit to recognize in Jesus the one sent by the Father for the salvation of the world. This community has kept the memory alive by preserving, cherishing and handing on from generation to generation the earliest records of Jesus, the words and acts of the earliest witnesses, and that body of writing which was sacred Scripture for the Jewish people and therefore for Jesus and his disciples and which tells the story for which the ministry of Jesus is the hermeneutic key. This whole corpus of writings has been recognized and accepted by the church as providing the norm by which subsequent developments in the interpretation of the Gospel and of its implications are to be tested.

The first communicators of the Gospel were the eyewitnesses who could say 'That which we have seen and heard ... we declare to you'. They were well aware that their story could be and would be rejected, and that only the word of the Holy Spirit could convince people of its truth. But they did not draw the conclusion that its truth was a private matter for the individual. They did not avail themselves of the protection which Roman law provided for the exercise of religions of personal salvation. They affirmed that the message which had been entrusted to them was one which concerned the destiny of the whole human race. The one who had died and risen again was the saviour and judge of the world. The news was of vital concern to every human being. It was public truth. Fidelity to it required the momentous decision to withhold acknowledgement of the emperor as supreme power. They accepted the price which had to be paid for this fidelity.

To affirm the Gospel as public truth does not mean, therefore, that belief in the truth of the Gospel is to be ensured by the use of political power. It has been made clear from the beginning, though often forgotten in subsequent centuries, that the form of the affirmation is given once and for all in the witness which Jesus bore in his dying. The fact that the cross is at the heart of the Gospel, and that it was the powers of state, church and popular opinion which sought to silence the divine word, must forever forbid the church to seek an identification of the Gospel with political power. But the Gospel, the good news with which the church is entrusted, is that God raised the rejected Jesus from the dead and that he is now alive and at work in the community which he sent forth to tell the story. This means that he is the rightful bearer of God's rule even though that rule is now veiled in weakness. With all its weakness, sinfulness and compromise, the church is the body entrusted with the responsibility of bearing witness to the fact that the one whom Jesus called Father is the Lord and will be the judge of all without exception. This is public truth.

In contemporary 'modern' culture, the model of public truth is to be found in timeless law-like statements, ideally capable of being stated in mathematical form. From its early roots in Greek thought this model has been powerful in European culture. Perhaps the most important example is to be found in the enormous influence of the work of Isaac Newton on the thinkers of the 'Age of Reason' in which modern Western culture was shaped. Since that time it has been common to identify 'public truth' with matters which can be stated in this form. The word 'scientific' is used to distinguish knowledge of this kind from claims to know which rest on faith. What is forgotten is that the entire 'scientific world-view' rests on assumptions which are accepted in faith but cannot be proved true otherwise than in the actual practice of science. To affirm the Gospel as public truth is to invite acceptance of a new starting point for thought, the truth of which will be proved only in the course of a life of reflection and action which proves itself more adequate to the totality of human experience than its rivals. To claim that the Gospel is public truth is, therefore, certainly not to seek some kind of dominance for the church. It is to embark on a journey of faith which looks for final justification only at the end. It is not to seek for the Gospel any coercive power in the arena of public debate but it is to insist that the Gospel must be heard as an affirmation of the truth which must finally govern every facet of human life. It is not to ask that the Gospel should exclude all other voices, only that it should be heard. The universal recognition that Jesus is Lord is something promised for the end, not for the present age.

To affirm the Gospel as public truth is not to assert dominance but to invite dialogue. The announcement of things which have happened is not the fruit of dialogue but its starting point, for the meaning and implications of what is announced have to be learned in dialogue. For news of things that have happened we depend upon competent witness. Dialogue is not a substitute for reliable information. The first responsibility of the church is to give faithful witness to the things that have happened. But this must lead on to dialogue, for the witnessing community does not know in advance what the message will entail, what will be the consequences of its acceptance in the several areas of human life. The New Testament itself shows that the church, as it moved out from its roots in Israel to all the nations, had to learn (and be surprised by) what the implications would be (e.g. Acts 10 and 11). In the same way the church has to learn what the implications of the Gospel might be for the worlds of (for example) economics, education and healing. This can only come about through dialogue in which, as Jesus promised, the church must learn new things (John 16.12–15). And it is important to remember that, in this same context, Jesus told his disciples that they must expect hostility and rejection. The church must not aspire to any other kind of authority than that of the crucified and risen Jesus. The final 'proof' of the thesis can only be at the end of history, at the final consummation of which the resurrection of Jesus is pledge and first-fruit.

Lesslie Newbigin served for many years as a missionary and bishop in the Church of South India. He has been deeply involved in international ecumenical affairs. His current concerns, outlined above, are now contained in several books beginning with *The Other Side of 1984* (1983).

The great divide

The Christian community is made up of those who should be bringing to the fore 'fundamental issues of common concern'. The Christian community consists of those who should be seeking to give expression to 'a new kind of faith' which might address those issues with new vigour and growing perceptiveness. The problem is that a 'great divide' has opened up between the private and the public, the sacred and the secular, church and world, which blocks real encounter and genuine exchange.

The emergence of this divide has forced the church in on itself so that the language and life-style of Sunday increasingly fails to connect with that of Monday. Many Christians, clergy and laity alike, have thus lost the ability to make connections between faith and daily life, not least in the context of the messiness of the many ethical decisions that have to be made in the confusion of the public domain. As a result a faith which is of universal significance is condemned to institutional captivity and is seen as little earthly use by many, including many Christians, in the hurly-burly of everyday life.

A public vision for society

George Carey

(Extracts from an address given to community leaders at Harrogate, 30 October 1992)

'Private' and 'public': what an unholy mess has our society made of these two concepts!

. . .

'Private' and 'public': what an unholy mess has our society made of these two concepts! In matters of morality what should remain private and intimate is too often made public. And what should be public is made private.

THE PRIVATE MADE PUBLIC

First, private matters made public. I believe that the constant marketing of explicit sex and human pain, in most cases purely for entertainment, nourishes an obsession with these aspects of life which is damaging. It may make irresponsible attitudes and dangerous behaviour more likely in society at large. For it detaches our experience of sex, pain or suffering from any context of love and respect for other people – and the weakening of that link can have dire consequences.

Surely, it is self-evident that the right to be alone, or with another person in private, is a fundamental aspect of individual freedom and essential to the growth of human personality. I am glad that it is recognized as a right in the European Human Rights Convention. Mere entertainment of others is not a sufficient reason to override it. We accept that this right is not absolute and must be weighed against the public interest, for instance in preventing crime or unmasking hypocrisy. Commercially-motivated intrusions on privacy through listening devices and telescopic cameras do, however, pose a serious potential threat to human dignity and rights . . .

THE PUBLIC MADE PRIVATE

One possible reason why there is now a tendency to treat private and intimate things as fair game for public entertainment is that morality is increasingly regarded as merely a matter of private concern. It is assumed that since there are no absolute standards to govern the good life, we might as well do what is right in our own eyes. Thus, what is good or evil is treated as a matter of individual opinion. Morality goes private. Religion becomes a matter for consenting adults in private if that happens to be their 'thing'. The purpose of life is relative to whatever an individual thinks, and nothing is absolutely good.

The privatization of morality has radically dangerous consequences at different levels. The individual, each of whom has the potential to reflect the goodness of God or the depths of evil, is vulnerable to unbridled selfishness and to a sense of futility and bewilderment if there is no absolute good and no absolute purpose of life. I sense that millions of our fellow citizens are struggling with the resulting spiritual emptiness.

It may be argued that many people have a strong, instinctive sense of values which is not explicitly articulated. I agree, but such instincts draw heavily on the shared values of social convention embedded in our culture. The weaker such explicit commitment to moral standards becomes, the weaker their influence will tend to be on the instincts of future generations.

Moreover, the cohesion of society is undermined. The sense of collective values and principles, binding people across barriers of class, race and region, has dwindled as our understanding of ultimate purpose and morality goes private. It then becomes more difficult for society to withstand the misfortunes of economic adversity and unemployment without conflict. Hence, I believe that the privatization of morality afflicts our political culture, as well as individual and family life. Beneath topical political problems relating to economic management or Europe lies a deeper confusion about what the moral purpose of society should be.

MORALITY IS INDIVISIBLE

For no government or legislature can divest itself of the responsibility to make moral judgements. Like it or not, virtually every market – whether we are talking about the Stock Exchange or the stalls in our local town each Saturday – is influenced or tilted by choices made by human beings, and those choices have an inescapable moral dimension. It is better if these choices are made consciously and, in a democratic society, explicitly. The chosen framework for market forces can, for example, make or mar the environment ... avoiding the choice is not a real option. Similarly, public policy determines the fate of prisoners and offenders, of refugees and immigrants, and what is taught in our schools. It determines how far we assist or turn our backs on people facing calamitous poverty and starvation overseas. It strongly influences the life-chances of different citizens, the stability of family life, the kind of behaviour which should be tolerated and which should be prohibited in the public interest. All these and many more are moral decisions. They can be taken by default or by choice, but they cannot be dodged. On what basis shall we take them if morality is privatized and if we abandon shared values? The answer is that we shall stumble about lacking any vision upon which to base the inescapable moral judgements of public policy.

. . .

TRUST

Central to the tension between the private and public worlds we live in is the concept of trust. I think we will agree that without trust free societies cannot survive. Without being starry-eyed, I think that as a nation we have been relatively fortunate in the extent which we have been able to trust the people in our key institutions to work honestly to serve the public interest. In each case, their legitimacy and effectiveness rests on that trust. Industrialists and bankers depend on it. The armed services depend on it. The police and criminal justice system depend on it. The Royal Family, the Civil Service, the medical and political establishments, the churches: none can flourish without the trust of the people that their leaders have an essentially moral purpose; that, whatever their weaknesses, they are trying to serve their fellow human beings, not just themselves; that self-interest is not unbridled but is harnessed to a wider good and is therefore honourable and acceptable. That is why trust relies on morality, on the recognition of purposes and standards beyond the individual's self-centredness. That is also why the privatization of morality, if it spreads through the institutions of society, will undermine the trust which the people place in them.

. . .

I believe we should set ourselves the ambition to roll back the privatization of morality, strengthen the trust of the people in key institutions and rebuild our collective confidence in the vision of a good society with shared moral purposes.

. . .

George Carey is the Archbishop of Canterbury.

Christians in public life: the theological challenge

Alistair McFadyen

The frames of reference we habitually employ as we analyse, interpret, communicate, judge and act in our public lives and work exclude any reference to God.

Virtually all Christians in a society like ours are engaged in public life in some way and at some level. That is manifestly the case. What is less clear, however, is how and to what extent our Christianity engages with, enters and shapes our public life and work. To what extent, one might ask, do we enter and engage in public life actually as Christians?

EXCLUSIVE FRAMES OF REFERENCE

I ask this question because, in our highly secularized culture, we find it immensely difficult to make connections between Christianity and the public world. Why is that? Because our culture has been immensely successful in developing powerful modes of explaining, understanding and acting in the world which are based on the world's integrity and independence from anything external to it. The frames of reference we habitually employ as we analyse, interpret, communicate, judge and act in our public lives and work exclude any reference to God. They are predicated on the assumption that, because there is no explicit and obvious presence of God in the public world (the material, institutional, social, economic, political), because the world has its own integrity, God is irrelevant to the tasks of interpreting, understanding and acting in it. God-talk and faith in God are sidelined along with God when it comes to the public domain. This is as true for Christians and members of other religious traditions as it is for atheists and agnostics. As civil servants, planners, social workers, neighbours, bankers, machinists, nurses, teachers – even if we live from a strong central core of faith in God – we adopt secular means of analysing, understanding, judging, acting. In public, then, we adopt frames of reference and action which are built on the assumption that God and the public world are, for all practical purposes, unrelated.

And is that, after all, not understandable, rational and right? What relevance have the trinitarian God, creation, incarnation, sin and salvation to community development work, running a business, administering a housing programme, alleviating poverty, healing the sick, or to understanding how the city works, what its pathologies are and how it might be humanized? We would surely rather turn to disciplines such as economics, human geography, sociology, medicine, political analysis, history, and to scientific and administrative technologies than to Christian faith, doctrine and theology. Because God has become disconnected from public discourses and practices in our culture, we find it hard to discern God's significance for our public lives and work, even if we live from a strong central core of Christian faith. One's faith appears to be irrelevant to the real business of public life. Living publicly appears to be a matter of exercising secular (pragmatically atheist) skills, understanding, wisdom, judgement, applying interpretive frameworks, techniques and technologies.

WITHDRAWAL

And so the existential situation of the Christian in public life is one in which there is a withdrawal of Christianity from the public world and from the cultural means whereby we inhabit it. Some Christians live this out in a fairly unambiguous dualism, in which the private sphere of personal beliefs and of churchiness are on one side; world and worldliness on the other. Very many others, however, experience their Christianity as having a more direct connection to their public life and work. Most typically, this is seen in terms of living by private, 'Christian' virtues in public life (e.g. honesty, probity and rectitude in professional dealings) or in terms of the Christian-inspired motivation to be involved in a particular form or sphere of public life. Whilst virtue and motivation enter public life, as a mode of connection between Christianity and the public world they remain yet on the personal side of the divide, rather than really bridging it. Through personal virtue and motivation Christianity may, indeed, make an impact on the public world, but it does so only indirectly and without making any difference to secular frameworks of understanding and acting which virtuous and motivated Christians are using (and, indeed, being shaped by in their public sensitivities).

What is true of individual Christians is true of corporate and institutional Christianity too. Beyond requiring a generalized sympathy with the Christian origins and ethos of the organization, both churches and Christian-founded agencies in practice generally require competence only in the secular skills appropriate to performing a given task. There is rarely any expectation that being a Christian or having the wisdom and skills of theological discernment would be of any practical use. Which is to say that God is expected to hold no explanatory power in relation to the public world, and so Christian faith and God-talk are supposed to make no positive difference to the way in which we interpret and act in it. Ironically, church reports on public issues also evidence this pulling apart of Christianity and public life. How many church reports begin with some explicit theology or biblical study which provides reasons for Christian concern in a particular area of social responsibility (closing perhaps with some theological reflection), but then analyse the issues in entirely secular (pragmatically atheist) terms? To all practical purposes the theological beginning and end are merely clipped on to a secular analysis which is unaltered by their presence. In this vein, it could be said that the *Faith in the City* (1985) report in fact spoke much more about faith *and* the city than faith *in* the city, setting them in parallel rather than as interacting.

DENYING A FUNDAMENTAL FRAME OF REFERENCE

All of this, in my rather arrogant view, evidences a massive failure on the part of both the churches and modern academic theology. For both have signally failed to find ways of speaking of God and world together. And so we verge on the abyss of giving up two essential, interrelated Christian affirmations. First, that the trinitarian God is intimately and dynamically present in, active in and related to the world. Second, that therefore the triune God is the ultimate explanation of everything, so that no explanation or mode of action may be adequate to the reality of the world or of human beings which excludes a theological referent. Where we give these affirmations up, we also give Christians up to pragmatically atheist ways of living in, acting in and interpreting the public world. We ensure that Christians will experience an alienation from their faith and from God in their public life and work. So this is a matter of immense practical significance, since it determines the extent to which Christians may experience and orient their public lives as related to the creative, sustaining and saving presence and action of God.

But what practical difference can Christian faith and God-talk make to living in the public world? It is clear that secular frameworks and disciplines have an essential place in discerning the truth about public life. But secular categories will prove inadequate, at the level both of description and of action, insofar as the secular remains Godless. Because, in the end, they are not in touch with the most fundamental structure and dynamic of reality, they are bound sometimes to offer us overly constrictive ways of construing and acting in public life, of what it means to humanize the city, say. No understanding or frame of action may be complete or adequate which fails to set reality in the context of God's creative and saving presence and action. We may only understand what is good and bad and why, when we see reality in their light. Without reference to God, we operate with a much restricted notion of the goals of humanization (absence of deprivation, of personal or social dysfunction, or inequality, or poverty, etc.) as well as of their means and of what can 'realistically' be expected. And so we need a brave and risky orthodoxy which helps Christians to see the ways in which their public life relates to the great drama of sin and salvation, to the presence and action of the trinitarian God and to worship of that God, and which enables those in public life to develop a distinctively Christian practical wisdom which they may practise in their public lives. For it is terms such as sin and salvation which bring most adequately to articulation: the dynamics operating in cities and in public life generally; the significance and possibilities of resistance to dehumanization; the possibilities of transformation – though often in small, fragmentary and fragile ways. And it is primarily worship which sustains hope and dignity and which mediates the vision and power of humanization in the city.

Alistair McFadyen is a lay Anglican. A senior lecturer in the Department of Theology and Religious Studies in the University of Leeds, he is the author of *The Call to Personhood* and is currently working on the doctrine of sin in relation to child sexual abuse and the Holocaust. He was a member of the Archbishop of Canterbury's Urban Theology Group and is currently a member of the Church of England's Doctrine Commission.

The churches and public affairs
Andrew Purkis

The churches' influence over public decision-taking has to be earned and nurtured.

. . .

CREDIBLE ENGAGEMENT

The churches' influence over public decision-taking has to be earned and nurtured. The light of the Gospel shines on all dimensions of life: yes, but that does not mean that the churches as institutions speak with equal authority on everything. They can speak with the weight of authentic pastoral experience about the realities of life and the actual effects of policies on real people on the ground. They can bring the distinctive gifts of theological reflection, prayer and church teaching to bear on defining moral goals and principles. But when it comes to the means by which desirable goals can be achieved, we need to acknowledge consistently that, as institutions, we have no special expertise. We often have no authoritative view on the likely economic, political or diplomatic success of different policy options. It should be no surprise that equally devoted Christians adopt quite contradictory views on these issues.

This is a distinction with blurred edges, but when official church pronouncements do not observe it at all and we do not stick to aspects of politics where churches have distinctive expertise, severe damage may be done to their credibility in public life. Quite a few church pronouncements still seem to position the churches as just another organization within the welfare and poverty lobby or imply pretty clearly that 'God votes Labour'.

If we affirm the relevance of our incarnational faith to people as politicians and citizens, the same affirmation must apply to people in business, offices, laboratories, in the uniformed services, wherever people carry their aspirations and strivings and try to do what is good. Here is a huge implied agenda for the churches. It is partly about 'owning' chaplaincies, sector ministries and voluntary organizations rather than treating them as self-contained initiatives separate from the 'real' church. It is partly about encouraging, and making connections with, Christian associations formed within workplaces and professions. It is partly about devoting more energies as church communities to forging links with local offices, factories, shops and services. What a transformation there would be if the time and effort spent on inward-looking church politics, rows over such matters as whether to use Rite A or Rite B and so forth, were devoted to outreach to people in their working lives!

Our liturgies and even our prayers still tend to be 'skewed' in favour of the domestic and caring aspect of life. There are some good initiatives in train to address this imbalance, but we need more.

CLARITY AND COMMUNICATION

There are yet more fundamental issues about how, from a church base, we can speak helpfully to the longings, joys and sorrows of people who do not go to church. It is hardly helpful if such people hear that we think they are damned, lost, deluded or wretched. We often give a muddled impression as to whether or not we believe God's grace and love is at work in the wider society and in people of all faiths and none. If we do, sharp questions arise about the priorities we give to affirming and strengthening what we believe to be good and pleasing to God in the wider society, or preaching Christian doctrine, winning converts and nurturing distinctive Christian communities.

The easy answer is that we should do all these things, but the question of priorities will not go away. Moreover, the special language of Christian doctrine and distinctive Christian communities may be puzzling and alienating to the un-churched and undermine our efforts to reach out to them and offer them love and support. It is so easy to forget how rapidly exposure to the language of 'Trinity ... Holy Ghost ... Incarnation ... Theology ... Heaven ... Last Judgement ...' and the like can convince conscientious people of good will that 'religion' is something separate, embodied in separate institutions called churches, and above all separate from the hopes and fears of their own lives.

Our controversies over doctrine, liturgy and church order reinforce this impression, and we forget that other people are listening.

On the other hand, if the substance of our contribution to debate is not perceived to be distinctive, to be an expression of Christian faith, we lose our special authority altogether. We become just one more not-very-weighty voice in a secular argument.

HOW ARE WE DOING?

So how are we working through these sharp dilemmas? How are we working out what our distinctive contribution is as churches, what our concerted messages should be and how they can be formulated in order to have the effect we want? On the whole, the answer is: 'not very well'. Most other interest groups in our society do it better. No doubt this is partly because of the dispersed nature of authority in most denominations. But it is also because of our own ambivalence about how far we as churches are part and parcel of the wider society, and how far we want to be separate and different just because we are religious. How easy it is, against this background, to behave like other marginalized groups estranged from mainstream society. We can justify almost any naïve or counter-productive pronouncement on the grounds that it is 'prophetic' (a favourite 'church-y' word). But what does this say about the nature of our separateness?

. . .

The implicit agenda for action, thinking and prayer is enormous and exciting. None of these challenges is more important than wrestling with the constant dilemmas of how distinctive, how separate and how 'church-y' we want to be in public life because we are Christian. These dilemmas are inherent in the very nature of the Christian revelation in which our Lord is both human and divine.

Andrew Purkis is the Archbishop of Canterbury's Secretary for Public Affairs.

The two cultures
Lois Green

Sharing the value and richness of Christian insights with those in public life is not a problem of intellectual credibility, but of cultural dissonance.

Sharing the value and richness of Christian insights with those in public life is not a problem of intellectual credibility, but of cultural dissonance. In the post-industrial society an increasing proportion of those economically active are 'knowledge workers', handling information, data and words rather than materials and products, who are often stimulated by new ideas and ideals. They might be quite open-minded or even in favour of a Christian viewpoint, if this did not immediately present them with a cultural chasm separating them from their working world. Anyone with the courage to straddle or jump this chasm deserves our support and encouragement.

As a busy knowledge worker who admits the supremacy of Christian belief, I would like to elaborate on these two cultures, though I realize the brevity of this paper precludes the qualifications which could be made to almost every statement. My aim is to seek resonance rather than complete agreement; to arouse echoes in the mind of the reader.

WORLDS APART?

- At work I am called upon to be innovative, creative and participative; at church to be passive, conforming and controlled.
- At work I am required to identify my strengths and seek recognition; at church to confess my weakness and claim forgiveness.
- At work there is often conflict, if not always of the aggressive kind; at church conflict is denied or suppressed.
- At work the role of the professional is being severely questioned; at church professionals are imbued with almost mystical powers.
- Work demands intense periods of intellectual and/or physical activity: church places emphasis on being rather than doing, on silence, contemplation and reflection.
- Work puts a value on logical thought convincingly articulated; the spiritual life has a point at which logic must cease and words are shown to be the dangerous things they are.
- Work demands 'performance measures' and is concerned with 'outcomes'; church puts emphasis on doing one's best and leaving the outcome to God.

Of course there are jobs which require quiet reflection, some bureaucratic work environments, and some enterprising churches. But my main point is that the culture of church and the culture of working life are so different as to create a barrier which few are motivated to remove. Instead, Christians in public life who feel they have something to say want to become lay readers or join the ordained ministry. Clergy request sabbatical years in industry getting artificial work experience.

THE CLERGY

1. Clergy have failed to capture the moral high ground in industrial relations because of the church's mediocre record as an employer.
2. They tend to see the world of work in terms of atomized skills and tasks, skills which they consider should be freely available for the service of the local church. For example, they perceive a bank manager as someone who will 'do the books' and a teacher as someone to take a Sunday school class, overlooking the interpersonal, planning and decision-making skills such people possess.
3. They cling to a model of the work situation which depicts it as stressful, monotonous and unfulfilling. They offer to give but do not expect to get. They could learn from management how to harness the skills and abilities of knowledge workers to fulfil given objectives, but they do not ask. When they claim to want management skills they usually mean some administrative technique, like budgeting, not realizing that a manager's task is not to run things but to change things.
4. They are often forced by their congregations into becoming instruments of control, conformity and continuity. There are intricate hierarchies both in the professional structure of the Church of England, and in the committee structures of Nonconformity: terms such as 'Steward', 'Elder', 'Pastor', 'Class Leader', 'Superintendent' all emphasize a control model.
5. At the time of a rapidly changing, disparate and mobile labour force, they still tend to equate working life with those employed in large-scale organizations. Even clergy who have made successful contacts with knowledge workers have difficulty in relating to other sectors of the economy. Growth areas within the economy at present are residential care, fast-food franchising, and security. Can the church be any more relevant to these workers than to the miners, dockers and steelworkers of previous eras?

THE LAITY

1. The laity often need the church to be a point of continuity in a changing life, and thus stifle innovation through a desire to escape.

2. They compartmentalize, keeping church and working life apart on the grounds that they want to be accepted for what they are, rather than what they do. Alternatively they assume that having achieved prominence in one sphere, they can legitimately dominate that of church affairs.

3. They like to promote their own image as men and women of the world by portraying the clergy as rather naïve. They often under-rate the clergy's managerial abilities and do not use them intelligently, demanding about 50 per cent of their intellectual ability and 200 per cent of their time.

4. They invest too much emotional capital in their dealing with the clergy so that rigorous discussion is replaced by dependency or aggression.

5. Those Christian groups which do exist within secular organizations and professions largely resemble special interest cliques rather than powerful change agents. The vast majority of lay people have passively accepted the secularization of public debate so that the Christian viewpoint is left to such extremists.

BRIDGE-BUILDING

The way through these problems may be very difficult to find but it has to do with enabling or empowering. It means the clergy enabling the laity to articulate their concerns, to make open choices and to use the resources particular to themselves. It means the laity developing for themselves an appropriate and holistic role in public life and requesting the clergy to help equip them for it.

The solution is not for each to take a long circuitous route to the other's camp, but to build bridges between the two cultures. Once the bridges are built there will be the opportunity of frequent and fruitful traffic across them and the common search for the meaning and purpose of being human can begin.

Lois Green was until recently a principal lecturer in the School of Information Studies at the University of Central England in Birmingham.

The search
David Clark

To keep asunder church and world is to promote idolatry.

> 'Are not the child-abusers also God's children?' (Residential child-care worker)'

> 'Being alongside people who are trying to make sense of words and to find words, is an enormous challenge but also a privilege.' (Teacher in a centre for recently arrived immigrant children)

> 'We are all stewards, holding our possessions in trust for God. Banking is no different.' (Bank official)

> 'The question I should be asking is "What in heaven's name am I here to do?"' (FE college lecturer)

These words from Christians active in public life remind us that the search to discover the nature of the Kingdom of God and to work for its fuller manifestation goes on every week and in every sector of our society. Christians from all denominations are in a myriad ways daily involved throughout our society in seeking to discern and bear witness to that Kingdom, present and to come.

The problem is not the lack of Christians deeply involved in this way in public life. It is that they are so often left by the church as an institution to undertake this task unrecognized and unsupported. Their struggles and their questions, their discoveries and their insights remain theirs and theirs alone – few affirm, listen to or learn about their work for the Kingdom in the world beyond the parish.

The community of faith from which, against heavy odds, they continue to draw some sustenance and inspiration has become locked into the private and the domestic realms of life, at home dominantly with the personal and the familiar. The public domain, where the stranger and the unfamiliar are regularly encountered, has become foreign and hostile territory. The church gathered is recognized, acknowledged and resourced; the church dispersed is unacknowledged, forgotten and adrift.

THE GREAT DIVIDE

This disengagement of the gathered church from the dispersed church, and thus of the church as institution from the wider life of society, is not only a denial of the Gospel's call that we seek, discern and proclaim the signs of the Kingdom. It means that both church and world are fatally impoverished. The church becomes a ghetto and the world a wilderness.

To put asunder church and world in this way is to deny that the whole of creation belongs to God. It is to refuse to recognize Christ incarnate in every part of that creation, redeeming and liberating all people. It is to reject the work of the Spirit, reconciling and sanctifying in every sphere of life, private and public.

To keep asunder church and world is to promote idolatry.

> 'One is living in a society which is basically not Christian in any really meaningful way.' (Director of a voluntary organization)

> 'In the very desperate situation we're in, I have to keep going in sometimes almost impossible circumstances.' (City planning officer)

For these Christians, secularism, the denial of God's rightful ownership, dominates the public scene. They feel themselves to be working in a world where God is not only unknown but unwanted. There will be many attempting to live out the life of the Kingdom in public affairs, but their beliefs are ignored, rejected and marginalized. A secular world turned in on itself asks few ultimate questions, is constantly prone to make absolute what is relative and to deify what is human. The consequences are manifest ... in every sector and institution of our society. For the world to sideline the community of faith means that hope and love also take a back seat.

> 'The church's effortless paternalism based on the assumption of an authority which it no longer holds, makes me wonder which century I'm living in.' (Homeworker)

> 'The fervent militancy, as well as brilliant business skills, of the fundamentalists scare me stiff.' (Councillor)

For these Christians, it is idolatry within the church which 'scares them stiff'. The 'community of faith' which disengages from God at work in the whole of his creation can know neither Kingdom nor King. Its energy is that of the ghetto, turned in on and destructive of itself, and its growth is stunted by the privatization of its faith and life. Sacralism, no less then secularism, denies a liberating and reconciling God entry into its affairs.

ACROSS THE DIVIDE

For ghetto and wilderness to lose their power to alienate and destroy, sacred and secular communities have to re-engage in a shared search for the Kingdom. This is a search as old as history itself. But its old forms are dead. The sacred world of Christendom and the secular world of the Enlightenment are now things of the past. The search for the Kingdom cannot get underway again until our captivity to both sacralism and secularism are ended. This means those active in public affairs, increasingly aware that human institutions have a potential for great evil as well as great good, are open to share with and listen to those whose beliefs and values might offer new insights and direction. It means that those who identify with the church, who are coming to acknowledge that no ghetto however sacred can hope to save itself or others, are ready to enter into a lively and open discourse with those whose experience of the signs of the Kingdom may be very different.

...

A new kind of mission

There is no blueprint for how the mission of the church should be undertaken. Bearing Christian witness has taken a myriad forms down the centuries. It has been shaped as much by the historical and cultural context as by how the nature of faith itself is understood. There remain many 'models of mission'.

But if for our generation 'a great divide' has opened up to separate church from world, then 'a new kind of faith', however important this be for the survival of humankind, will necessitate 'a new kind of mission'. Without the latter, Christian and non-Christian will be unable 'to engage, share and work together ... in addressing fundamental issues of common concern' (Christians in Public Life's stated purpose).

At the heart of a new kind of mission lies the belief that the transformation of our world, its re-creation through the power of the Trinity, can only begin through the process of dialogue. Such dialogue is not the abandonment of conviction or passion, but both these energizing an open-minded and open-hearted encounter with others in search of a deeper understanding of God and his purposes in our day and age.

This kind of mission will require of many Christians not only a profound change of stance in relation to the 'secular' world, but recognition of the need for a new language which will enable us to speak empathetically and meaningfully to women and men in this post-modern age.

Models of mission

David Clark

Models ... to prevent us from assuming that there is only one genuine model of mission.

Kaleidoscopes are fun – ever more sophisticated – often computerized. Shake them and the patterns are amazingly beautiful. But never the same twice.

We live in a kaleidoscopic world. Of course, cultures and customs, rituals and symbols of bewildering diversity have always existed. But now they are brought continuously together into one global kaleidoscope which is constantly shaken to bring us 'the picture for the day'. No wonder that as Christians trying to relate our faith to daily life, the ever changing kaleidoscope of human affairs, from the local to the international scene, leaves us bemused and bewildered. What are we trying to communicate? To whom? Where? How? When?

Our confusion is made worse by the diversity of terms theologians have used to describe this task – 'mission', 'witness', 'evangelism'. We even have two words for the ten years of effort into which we have ... entered – 'the Decade of Evangelism' and/or 'the Decade of Evangelization'... Set out overleaf is an attempt to begin to address this problem – seven 'models of mission' which may at least help us take stock, get our bearings. They are offered, first and foremost, to prevent us from assuming that there is only one genuine model of mission – of course mine! – and, therefore, all the other approaches must be 'wrong' or 'inadequate'. Secondly, they are presented to suggest that different approaches to mission may be complementary – not in conflict. Perhaps those of us committed to 'negotiation' need to recognize that 'liberation' is important too, those of us engaged in 'socialization' to affirm the significance of 'conversion'. And, thirdly, the models may remind us that our approach to mission has to be related to the cultural or political social context in which we find ourselves – we have to be 'men and women for all seasons'.

Models can be misleading, even dangerous, if we use them to 'label' or, worse still, 'stereotype' our fellows. The reality is that we all mix together bits of different models, and others not listed here, as and when we choose – for we are unique persons in unique situations. Nonetheless, the patterns of mission set out may help us to 'locate the options' or 'ring the changes' with a little more thoughtfulness and empathy than is the case at present.

MODELS OF MISSION

	Socialization	Conversion	Ministration	Demonstration	Liberation	Negotiation	Exploration
Direction	(arrow)	(arrow)	(arrow)	(arrow)	(arrow)	(arrow)	(arrow)
	(Church)	(Church)	(Church/World)	(World)	(World)	(Neutral)	(Unknown)
Target group	Young people	Sinful people	Needy people	Attentive people	Oppressed people	'Other' people	Enquiring people
Purpose	To incorporate/induct	To change/reform	To affirm/care for	To impress/influence	To free/emancipate	To share/discuss	To question/discover
Process	Initiation/confirmation	'Evangelism'	Service	'Presence'	'Conscientization'	Dialogue	Journey/quest
Slogan	'One of the family'	'Born again'	'Help along the way'	'Bread upon the waters'	'Option for the poor'	'Cards upon the table'	'In search of the Holy Grail'
Authority	Tradition	Bible/experience	Tradition/experience	Experience	Bible/experience	Tradition	Experience
Outcome sought	Belonging	Repentance/renewal	Well-being	Awareness/interest	Justice/peace	Mutual understanding/partnership	'Ultimate truth'
Role of leader	'Parent'/teacher	Preacher/'evangelist'	Pastor/'servant'	Example/model	Prophet/animator	Mediator/representative	Pioneer/explorer

Models of mission – transformation

David Clark

Without 'transformation' mission is literally 'hopeless'.

In the preceding paper, I set out seven models of mission. But I do not want to leave the impression that the mission of Christians in public life is simply a pick and mix affair, a matter of purely personal choice depending on our personal temperament or current mood. So here I offer an eighth model – 'Transformation'. It is one which I believe should particularly guide and fashion our mission as Christians in public life.

TRANSFORMATION

Of course the mission of Christians in public life is about 'socialization' (nurturing newcomers in the faith), 'conversion' (proclaiming the good news of personal salvation) and 'ministration' (caring for the needy). Of course such mission will involve us in 'demonstration' (as 'significant others'), in 'liberation' (speaking the truth in love) and 'negotiation' (seeking out the ultimate purpose of life together). But without 'transformation' mission is literally 'hopeless'. Transformation is about hope: hope in the midst of the strains and stresses of family life, hope in the hospice, hope in the dole queue, hope in the face of racial prejudice and bigotry, hope in the future of Hong Kong and Russia, hope for peace in Bosnia and Somalia. If we as Christians in public life are not hope-bearers, messengers of the promise of transformation, then let us pack our bags and get back into our private worlds of make-believe security as speedily as is respectable.

Transformation is the creation of 'a new heaven and a new earth'. It is a mind-blowing undertaking. But what else can possibly suffice in a world constantly threatening to push the self-destruct button – economically, militarily, demographically and ecologically. Our God is too small – tribalized, domesticated, depersonalized, marginalized. If we as Christians are to bring God-given hope to a 'God-forsaken' world then the agenda can be nothing less than transformation.

DIRECTION

This transformation is of world and church – we are all in it together. To fulfil our mission as Christians in public life is not a call to 'come hither' and forget

Title	Transformation
Direction	(Church/World)
Target Group	All people
Purpose	To make whole
Process	Re-creation
Slogan	'Your Kingdom come'
Authority	Experience engaged with tradition and the Bible
Outcome sought	The Kingdom Community
Role of leader	Partner/co-creator

the world, or 'go thither' and ignore the church. Transformation is about church and world in partnership, searching out the means to be transformed into what God wants us to be. There can be no salvation of the church whilst the world remains untransformed; no salvation of the world whilst the church is not transfigured. If we forget transformation, the church will become our prison, the world our wilderness.

TARGET GROUP

The message of transformation is for all people – not just 'the young', 'the sinful', 'the needy', 'the oppressed' or 'the enquiring'. That we are called in public life to pay very special attention to the marginalized, to put the poor at the top of our agenda, remains a divine imperative. But transformation is where we all come in. For some of us it is about the end of deception, for some about the rebuilding of family life, for some about adequate food and shelter, for some about a new deal in business affairs, for some about openness in management, for some about a refashioned Europe or a new South Africa. Transformation is never just for 'them' and for 'those', it is for all of us.

PURPOSE AND PROCESS

Transformation is the realization of wholeness. This means starting where we are – not dodging realities or being naïve about the massive challenges we face – and moving on from there. For God's wholeness is not the negation of our uniqueness – individually or collectively – but the fulfilment of the promise of our lives whoever we are.

Transformation into wholeness never ends. It means being 'changed from glory into glory', ever more fully sharing the presence of God, here and beyond death. It always remains a corporate, not an individual destiny.

We are transformed – personally and publicly – by a process of re-creation, a passionate and explosive renewal and exchange of life, the work of God the Creator, Christ the Liberator and the empowering love of the Spirit, in dynamic 'pairing' and partnership. It is a process characterized by terms such as 'redemption' and 'rebirth', the bringing into being of 'a new heaven and a new earth'.

Such transformation is about the establishment of new and life-giving relationships which confront the death-dealing denial of women and men as human beings, be that as refugees at the airport, as unemployed in the job centre, as 'failures' in the classroom, as women in the church or as 'the opposition' in government. That the promise of transfiguring re-creation has not been purchased cheaply should only increase our amazement and thankfulness.

SLOGAN AND OUTCOME

There is only one 'slogan' and one outcome to the process of transformation. As those called Christians declare most Sundays, our mission statement is 'Your Kingdom come'. Not my kingdom, or our kingdom but that Kingdom whose 'King' has a real name and a real face, Christ Jesus. That Kingdom, that 'reign of the Lord' prepares us for 'the Kingdom Community', a realm of transformed relationships in which the devastating divides of our untransformed world begin to break down, in which healing takes place and wholeness becomes a reality.

The Kingdom Community is not a final destination but an ongoing process of becoming whole, individually, corporately and cosmically. As such, the Kingdom Community is constantly changing. Because change always requires new perspectives and insights, it is pre-eminently a learning community. Such learning is not just life-long but 'eternal life-long'.

AUTHORITY AND THE ROLE OF LEADERS

Our authority for being hope-bearers in public life comes from our experience of the gift and Giver of hope. That experience, as with all life-giving relationships, is born out of active and intimate encounter with God in our world – our public world – today. It is an experience shaped by our engagement with our forebears in the faith, and fashioned by a cross-cultural dialogue with the hope-bearers of the Bible.

The authority to be engaged in the divine work of transformation is rooted in love, the love of God who first loved us so that we might love one another. It is a love which, springing from both the Fatherhood and Motherhood of God, gives birth to new life and the unquenchable hope such birthing brings. Our task as 'leaders' is to share with others in public life that love which has first transfixed, then transformed us. Our role is that of partners and co-creators with the Trinity in the re-creation of church and world as the Kingdom.

The journey in and the journey out
The mission of Christians in public life
David Clark

The missionary journey is, for the Christian, both a journey in and a journey out ... The Kingdom 'within' and the Kingdom 'without' are two aspects of the one journey.

. . .

THE JOURNEY IN AND THE JOURNEY OUT

Making known the Kingdom entails an ongoing search, a journey. It is not a prescribed 'truth' which we possess and deliver to the misguided or ignorant. Mission is a process of discovery and declaration which demands as much from the Christian in public life as any friends or strangers met along the way.

This 'missionary journey' is, for the Christian, both a journey in and a journey out. In all the emphasis that is here being placed on Christians in public life, the development and enrichment of our private life remains essential. Indeed, like the picture of the goblet which suddenly 'switches' to become two faces as foreground changes to background, and then 'switches' back again, so for the Christian the journey in and the journey out take it in turns to assume pride of place. However, the journey cannot remain for too long inward or outward. The Kingdom 'within' and the Kingdom 'without' are two aspects of the one journey. Private needs public as much as public private. To separate the two is to make the journey as a whole an impossible undertaking.

The mission of Christians in public life is to draw on the experience of the inward and outward journeys so that the Kingdom is made known through the dispersed as fully as the gathered church. Within the latter the company of fellow-travellers is familiar, the times of meeting are frequent and the language is meaningful. For the dispersed church, however, it is 'a company of strangers' who are often encountered, meeting is often infrequent and the language has few religious 'handles'. But the journey in and the journey out, because they are part of one journey, embrace three common features which form the essence of mission, all verbs – to engage, to discover and to declare.

TO ENGAGE

There can be no mission to public life, no declaration about the Kingdom, unless Christians have experienced at first-hand the personal power of love exchanged. The People of the Way have to come to know for themselves the One who is 'the Way, the Truth and the Life' before they can make him known to others. The journey in is about discovering the power and passion which infuses the relationship between Christ and his true followers; enabling them to disperse into often hostile territory with confidence and courage.

The journey in has to be a real journey. It is about a real encounter with a real person which builds a real relationship. In Martin Buber's terms (1958), the journey in has to be an 'I–Thou' engagement for it to provide the impetus needed for the journey out. It is an encounter built from a living spirituality which offers Christians a deep sense of identity and purpose in their missionary task.

The journey out does not leave that relationship behind. As Harvey Cox (1965) puts it: 'The Kingdom of God, concentrated in the life of Jesus of Nazareth, remains the fullest possible disclosure of the partnership of God and man in history.' As Christians move into public life – from the office to the factory, the school to the hospital, the bus queue to the council chamber – they travel as partners with a King whose Kingdom they are to make known.

The journey out also means real engagement. Even if here it is a company of strangers who are encountered and relationships are often more of an 'I–You' than 'I–Thou' kind, this does not mean the depersonalizing of people. The mission of Christians in public life is founded on an exchange of love, whose model is the ministry of Christ, where strangers are listened to, affirmed, related to in a way that acknowledges their unique value – far more than many sparrows – in the scheme of things. Love can be exchanged through the word of encouragement, the generous donation, the smile, the stepping aside to help for a moment, and the patient waiting, as fully as through other more intimate relationships.

TO DISCOVER

Mission in public life is founded on seeking and finding the Kingdom, itself rooted in real engagement with real people. We cannot declare what we have not discovered for ourselves. To discover means to learn. When Christians cease learning, the Kingdom ceases to be the Kingdom. Mission is aborted.

Discovering more about the King and the Kingdom is always a breakthrough; a lateral shift, a 're-framing' of experience, a liberation. It means that which blocks the exchange of love is suddenly overcome or circumvented – light dawns, hope is kindled and power flows. It happened time and again as Christ drew people into 'upside-down thinking', as Charles Handy (1990) puts it. Christ was the master of the everyday story and the acted parable which opened up new worlds, which compelled a radical break with the old way of life and revealed a new dimension to the journey.

The journey in is an 'Aha! experience' – 'That's it!' 'Now I see!' It is about being 'surprised by joy', not as a self-indulgence but as giving impetus to the journey out. Yet we can never possess the final vision. The journey in never ceases because what we discern is always the next view around the next turn in the road.

The journey out is, likewise, a discovery of the Kingdom, only this time in the wider world – the private always interacts with the public, each giving perspective to the other. It may be discerning Christ on 'the high ground' of the academic quest for 'truth'. It may be discovering him in the homeless and the hungry. But the discovery is always a breakthrough, a surprise, an unblocking of the channels which allow love to flow. And, as with the journey in, such discerning of the Kingdom means that life can never be the same again. 'The Kingdom of God is upon you; repent ...' – turn, change and begin the next stage of the journey. To discover the Kingdom is to be faced with a radical decision – about politics and economics as much as personal morality and behaviour. It is to 'come of age', to have to take responsibility for our lives and our world, public as well as private.

TO DECLARE

To make known the Kingdom in public life is, for Christians as much as others, a process of real engagement with people and of openness to learn. But it has also to be a response – a readiness to stop hiding candles under tubs and to make known what is hidden.

The journey in is about the requirements of the Kingdom becoming known to ourselves. It is about clarifying what 'calling', 'vocation' and 'mission' mean for us in our particular time and place. It is about not pretending, letting go the God in whom we no longer believe and welcoming the God who believes in us (as a prayer from Iona puts it). The journey in is not an endless quest for some holy grail, for a remote 'perfection', but to discover what Christ is asking us to be and do as People of the Way. Whether that doing is more active or passive is not the point. The point is that engagement and discovery require from us a down-to-earth response which in some way helps to make the Kingdom more fully known.

The journey out is to set our 'vocation' in a wider context. This may at times be about proclaiming the good news in words – 'speaking the truth in love'. Though assuredly in this context we shall need a new language and new symbols. But the Kingdom will also be made known in a wide diversity of other ministries focused around the struggle for justice, reconciliation, healing.

What matters is not the forms through which love is exchanged but that they make manifest the nature of the Kingdom, that they offer signs of the Kingdom to be recognized and responded to. What is happening on the journey out is our taking the ordinary and making it extraordinary, the re-creation and re-presentation of the everyday as a channel of God's love. It is a priestly role, the taking and breaking of the stuff of daily life so that it can reveal the 'real presence' of Christ the King. It is a 'priesthood of all believers'.

The exchange of love is at the heart of mission. Such an exchange is passionate or there can be no breakthrough into new life and new worlds. Passion means excitement, energy and sometimes violence – so will the Kingdom of God come. But it also means waiting and watching, and sometimes suffering. For those who are the People of the Way, as with Christ the Way himself, passion in all senses will be present. But Christ's Passion heralded the triumph of the Kingdom once and for all, and to that amazing truth Christians in public life also bear witness.

Mission as dialogue
Kevin Walcot

The mission of the church has to be seen as an ever widening dialogical process between the church, one of God's peoples, and the rest of creation.

MISSION AS PROBLEM

'Mission', says Walter Hollenweger, 'no longer has problems. It is a problem.' There is abundant evidence for this in the declining contributions to mission societies, lower recruitment rates to mission bodies, increased awareness of the riches of other religious traditions and a troubling awareness that we are not needed by our vibrant sister churches of the two-thirds world in the way we once believed we were. Until the Decade of Evangelism or Evangelization, churches in Britain felt they could comfortably shrug off mission and mission studies as not primarily their concern.

Slowly, however, perceptions have changed, for the Decade has brought controversy and confusion: what is evangelism/evangelization, to whom is it directed, by whom is it to be undertaken, what methods are to be used, should it be called evangelism or renewal? Inter-faith activity and reflection are no longer seen as quite so marginal, especially when they pose questions central to the very heart of Christian theology.

. . .

But it is not only the theological questions raised by the now commonplace encounters among people of faith in Britain to traditional Christian theology that is significant but also the quality of these encounters. The very nature of the two-way relationships which are being formed poses its own questions about our understanding of mission and who needs whom. Added to this are new insights into the life of Jesus as a universal model of self-giving, vulnerable communication (a Vatican document has described communication as 'the giving of self in love') and contributions from missiology. Taken together, these suggest that mission is the responsibility of all Christians, arising out of baptism and not from ecclesial commission; that it is from everywhere to everywhere but that geography is not the only or even principal consideration; that there are un-evangelized spaces as well as un-evangelized places; that many of our absolutes have been relativized by our greater understanding of cultural differences. Above all, mission is understood as a dialogical relationship between Christians, people of other faiths and ideologies, and people of no faith.

MISSION AS DIALOGUE (DIALOGICAL RELATIONSHIP)

I would suggest here, then, that the mission of the church has to be seen as an ever widening dialogical process between the church, one of God's peoples, and the rest of creation. But the crux of the matter is that dialogue between the church and the world cannot have credibility unless there is dialogue within the church itself. So the equality of the two partners to the dialogue that is assumed for external dialogue has to be assumed for internal dialogue as well. This is no more than saying that a hierarchical, ministerial church structure has to be seen as the servant of the community. The church is essentially not hierarchy but community, a community in which each has her/his own role which is to be affirmed and respected, but is not to become a base for the exercise of power; for power and dialogue do not go together. This may be a commonplace of theology but unless it is practised and seen by the rest of humanity to be practised, the Decade and indeed the whole future of the church and its mission will be paralysed from within.

Such a dialogue needs to encompass the damaged relationship between humanity and nature, men and women, the world's diverse cultures, belief systems and ideologies, the sciences and humanities, economics and law, medicine and psychiatry, politics and finance, among others.

Since some cultures and belief systems have coped with some questions better than others there is need for mutual listening to, and learning from, other faiths; e.g. primal religions could have taught us much about relationships with nature had we not been so convinced they were primitive people who had nothing to offer us. Learning unbelief in our own infallibility may be our first step to wisdom.

So in each case the church will have much to learn, and perhaps much to teach, but having been so convinced of its teaching role for so long, and this teaching role having been so allied to a misconceived power role, a moratorium on teaching might be a healthier way forward. People might be constrained to listen when they perceive us as listening, the role model of Jesus as learner might be offered as a necessary complement to that of Jesus the teacher.

For some ... this might mean the church militant becoming the church hesitant, and perhaps not before time ... Ditching the vocabulary of the church militant (campaign, crusade, etc.) would seem to be a moral imperative; for we have seen all too clearly in these decades of reflection after the Holocaust just where Christian militancy can lead. Engaging the mind, the heart and the memory before opening the mouth seems sound advice for the church as for the rest of humanity. Far better to live with the taunt of hesitancy than face the judgement of preparing the ground for religious intolerance and even genocide.

But in any case, the church hesitant may yet become as sweet a sound as the church militant and triumphant used to be to our ears. It need not mean the church somnolent. It might do much to reverse the trend toward the church irrelevant and, one might be optimistic enough to believe, it might set the church on a course which could prevent it from becoming (for vastly different reasons well beyond the scope of this paper) the church insolvent!

MISSION IN JESUS' WAY

Fr Donal Dorr has pointed out in a recent unpublished article that Jesus' own understanding of his mission was neither a task imposed on him from outside, nor a self-appointed task, but his willing acceptance of what was already implied in his incarnation, his being a member of a particular family, his solidarity with a particular community and with the human race as a whole. From this flows a need for us likewise to understand our mission as our own responsibility for, and solidarity with, one another.

Thus Jesus did not receive a command from his Father which he then passed on as a command to his apostles and thence to the whole church. Seeing mission as something we are ordered to do to others rather than as a loving relationship we are invited to enter into with others has made us feel guilty about not entering into a great task. Feeling an obligation has led us to look for Scripture texts to support a mission that is commanded, and of course there is to hand the great commission in Matthew 28.19 to bolster our sense of need to obey and enter into the global task of converting the world. This in turn has led us into a kind of fundamentalism, isolating this one verse from the entire biblical tradition to support our need to be busy and to be needed.

Maintaining the response to the great commission as the only way of doing mission has led us to have a one-way, one-eyed or monological view of the relationship: they need us, we must respond; they are ignorant, we have the answers; they are poor, we have resources. We are thus back to a power-based sense of mission which completely overlooks our own poverty, our own ignorance and our own need. There is ample biblical support for an understanding of mission that is a never-ending dialogue, a reciprocal relationship based on being, loving solidarity, freedom and invitation rather than on doing, being needed, guilt, duty and compulsion.

THE CHALLENGE TO THE CHURCH OF THE DIALOGICAL IMPERATIVE

Despite a steadily growing appreciation of the gospel call to a dialogical approach to mission few seem to appreciate what a radical, even subversive notion a dialogical relationship with people represents, and what enormous demands it will continue to make on all of us, not least those in leadership roles within the church. For what Muslim or Hindu could possibly be interested in a dialogical relationship with a Christian community in which dialogical relationships between leaders and followers, men and women, theologians and bishops, priests and laity were not the order of the day? Jesus himself provides the model, highlighted in Luke 4 where an attempt is made on Jesus' life.

. . .

Our problem is basically that we will not embrace that vulnerability, will not take that risk. But the challenge to us all will never go away.

Some will always feel that they have not been missionary if they have not 'proclaimed' Christ. But we must surely err in thinking this has to be a monologue, when it could be a witnessing to our faith by our life and above all in our loving reciprocal relationships with others. Witness is martyrdom, *martyrion,* a new kind of self-imposed martyrdom, to our own preconceptions, to our deeply felt need to be needed, to the discipline of letting go, to risk and vulnerability. Bonhoeffer reminded us that there is no cheap grace. The cost of discipleship is the cost of change: to understand better both Jesus' sense of mission and our own.

Kevin Walcot was formerly Provincial of an international Roman Catholic Missionary Society. He has since resigned from active ministry and lives in Australia where he continues to pursue his interest in mission and dialogue.

Doing theology in public life
Elizabeth Templeton

Only if we really trust theology to emerge out of the interstices of our most widely shared living, and not in the closets of our religious affiliations, have we any hope of achieving theology as a dimension of public life.

It seems, on the surface, a long time since the days when you could not get a haircut or a loaf of bread in Antioch, because the barber and the baker were deep in heated debate as to the two natures of Christ! Nowadays, if you say you do theology, people often blink, check nervously that you said 'theo-' not 'geo-': and edge a little further along their seats as if poised for rapid retreat if need be. The Harold Wilson use of the term, to mean arid speculative stuff which has no bite on reality, has acquired near-dictionary status. Even in the churches, many see theology as something of a handicap, complicating 'simple' faith and piety, certainly not good for the punters, and at best the curious interest of a few rarefied souls.

IT IS HAPPENING

Yet beneath or behind this surface, I have the sense that there is a level of animation about theological questions which can often hardly articulate itself or name itself as that. Recently, for instance, I was asked to make some theological input to an in-service day for counsellors in training. The organizer warned me that I should take no dogma for granted, since the range of responses in the group would run from fairly orthodox Roman Catholic to a kind of New Age spirituality, with at least one person who would call herself out-and-out atheist.

We decided to explore the range of positions they might find held by coun-selling clients as to how God acted in the world; and to compare and contrast that with any view they themselves held. This was done initially by asking them to do a fast gallop through a questionnaire about whether they thought it possible or not that God could directly change things in the physical world or the psychological world; how they saw prayer, and the maturity or im-maturity of those who prayed for specific outcomes or solutions; and what ele-ments of the existing world they would classify as evil. On the 18 questions asked, there was a maximum range of 90 answers. To everyone's amazement, this group of about 20 people 'filled' 85 of the available responses to the themes. It was hardly difficult, then, to spend the rest of the day in conversa-tion and reflection, trying to map the implications of this vast range of judge-ment, belief, imagination and expectation. And at the end of five hours of what was clearly doing theology, people were amazed to discover that they had participated with no difficulty and they had enjoyed themselves.

Or again, a year or two ago, when I acted locum in our local church for three months, I invited people to write down questions or issues they would like to see tackled in sermons. So many good, sharp, wrestling questions came – particularly on suffering and evil – that I could have preached through a year of Sundays on the strength of them. I was certainly given ample material for the whole of Lent which was 'owned' by far more people than would have felt the same way about any Lent agenda I could have devised.

REALIZING THE POTENTIAL

Somehow, over decades, people who are thoughtful, literate and competent in other spheres like politics, childcare or artistic judgement have been pauperized theologically, and deprived of the tools for mature reflection on faith issues. One cannot easily identify malice aforethought in this, any deliberate will to disinherit people. But, certainly, there has been some kind of slow strange col-lusion in keeping people in the dark!

. . .

So within the public life of the Christian and edge-of-Christian community, I am sure that we need a steady, strong educational confidence to nurture and maintain such potential for theological literacy.

WHAT IS 'BELIEF IN GOD'?

The harder question is how to do theology in that area of public life where no structure of explicit belief exists any longer, that is in the genuinely secular world of popular British and West European culture. Here a much greater effort of imaginative thought is needed, because God language has become an irretrievable code for so many. My own view is that all churches need to work harder at de-coding. That means two things. In the first place, it involves a real effort to identify what it means to 'believe in God' if you are, for some reason, robbed of the word. What is the phenomenology of believing? Once you are in the habit of using the language, that, of course, appears to structure experience in the 'obvious' ways suggested, for instance, by the language of prayer. But what is actually going on? Is it a distinctive set of discrete experiences which some people have and can compare, but not others? Is it a kind of ethical intuition? Is it a range of political commitments aligned with a certain core-reference to Jesus and the style of his life? Beyond the mere fact that you say the words, what difference does it make whether you believe in God-as-Trinity or in the God of Islam? What kind of an act is worshipping?

For religious believers to open themselves with candour to such questions might cause some consternation, but I am sure that until we in the churches can internalize such questions, we will not begin to address the yawning gulf between faith/belief and the secular world.

PAYING ATTENTION TO THE SECULAR

Yet precisely as we do that, I suspect, the yawning gulf will close. For as Christians learn to dismantle their complacencies of language, and to test them against the questions of a world which finds the language entirely strange, we may begin to pay more attention to other people's accounts of their experience.

That is the other major challenge for theology, and one which it has hardly undertaken with any constancy since Bonhoeffer (1953) so tantalizingly issued it in his *Letters and Papers from Prison*. It is to pay attention to the given (secular) vocabulary of the environment, and to notice how, via that, it articulates its own joys, fears, pains, solidarities and so on. Then, without necessarily doing any formal translation into religious terminology, to discern, to disseminate, to affirm, to participate in what actually is 'for good', 'of God', in all that, and to work in critical solidarity with the non-religious other as a way of earning the right to challenge where that seems called for. But both affirmation and challenge need to be delicate, unsuperior, unpatronizing, waiting to be surprised by the encounter.

My hope and confidence is that the recovery of a place for theology in public life will not depend on a re-animated religious sphere of existence, still polarized against secular life. And my appraisal of most religious revivals, associated so often with various fundamentalisms, is dark and uncomfortable. For me, the search for a public language, to bear a public debate about truth, has still hardly begun, because the churches exist, on the whole, inside a barricaded language rarely exposed to outside scrutiny. And the world has lost, on the whole, all expectancy of connection between its life and the churches, except in the vaguest of predictable ethical alignments.

'CONVERSATIONS-IN-RELATION-TO-LIFE'

It may be that straws begin to blow in an opposite breeze ... But what will emerge if we manage to enter the next century as dialogue-partners with our own culture, alert, undefensive and flexible in the business of hearing and attending, is anyone's guess. My hunch is that it will be creative, but only if we have no hidden agendas for surreptitious conversion. Only if we notice with no panic that in the voices of our contemporary creative arts, all the running is made by those whose idioms are secular. Only if we really trust theology to emerge out of the interstices of our most widely shared living, and not in the closets of our religious affiliations, have we any hope of achieving theology as a dimension of public life. That involves generosity and reticence and fearlessness in a rare combination. But any hope of a lively interaction between faith and the big wide pluralist world will depend upon it.

The modest starting agenda has to be finding, consolidating, and perhaps creating contact-points, clusters, networks, where such open searching conversations-in-relation-to-life can happen. That might be our equivalent to the more dramatic witnesses to faith which sometimes catch the eye, but do not always penetrate far below the surface. We can no longer scold, nag or bully the world into listening to 'us'. Giving ourselves the space and time to learn to speak polyphonically is our only chance to earn credibility.

Elizabeth Templeton works as Development Officer for the Christian Education Movement in Scotland. She does freelance work in the field of adult theological education.

PART II

Changing church

For Christians in public life seriously to engage with others in addressing the fundamental issues of our time, not only will a new understanding of faith be required but a form of mission which can span 'the great divide' which currently separates church from world. Such profound shifts of understanding and approach will in their turn require little short of a new 're-formation' in the life and organization of the church.

This second group of papers explores some of those changes that may be required of a church which is genuinely to engage with today's world.

The vocation of the People of God

There may be a great divide separating church and society as such, but millions of Christians are daily crossing that divide simply because of their family, work and leisure commitments. How then can a greater awareness of their identity as a Christian community help to bring the insights and resources of faith to bear on the key issues of today's world? The answer has everything to do with a deeper understanding of their calling as the People of God.

Lay vocation – the call to becoming persons

David Clark

Lay vocation ... is about a shared call and mutual response to personhood, individually and communally.

RECLAIMING 'VOCATION'

We must ... reclaim the word 'vocation' for the whole ministry of the whole People of God. 'Vocation', as a once potent religious concept, has been hijacked in two very destructive ways. On the one hand, it has been 'commercialized' by being limited to only those forms of work which can lead to paid employment. Thus a host of marketable 'national vocational qualifications' are being designed which relegate 'non-vocational' interests and skills to the back burner. On the other hand, an élitist dimension to the idea of 'vocation' still lingers on when it is applied to the so-called professions – teaching, medicine, law and the church (meaning only the clergy of course) – set aside as special and respected forms of public service located within the particular institutions concerned.

These interpretations of vocation are both debilitating and divisive. They limit the term to a restrictive range of competences or to an exclusive group of people. Vocation in this sense is about achievement not commitment, about the status of the few not the potential of the many. In brief, vocation becomes a restrictive practice, not an inclusive calling.

For the liberation of the church to occur, we need to reclaim the word 'vocation' for the whole People of God. This is not to exclude the ordained or the religious orders, but to argue that the vocation of the laity is crucial to the mission and ministry of the church. Their calling is not secondary or subsidiary to that of the clergy, it is just as important and equally valid. Indeed, if we do not reinstate lay vocation to its proper place in the life of the church, continuing institutional decline and demise are inevitable.

PARTNERSHIP

Lay vocation is first and foremost a call to partnership; the biblical word is covenant. CIPL's 'statement of conviction' puts it this way:

> We are called to be partners with God in his continuing work of creation within the personal, corporate and global spheres of life.

We are called to be partners with Christ as he frees and empowers individuals, institutions and nations to fulfil their God-given possibilities.

We are called to be partners with the Spirit as she works for justice, peace and the unity of humankind.

We are called to be partners with all those who work to further human dignity within the bounds of our common humanity.

Such a calling is not so much to doing as to being. Alistair McFadyen, in his very important work with the same title (1990), describes this as *The Call to Personhood*. God first calls you and me, through an I–Thou relationship with him, and through the 'exchange of life' which goes with that, to realize the gift of our human possibilities. Lay vocation means that we are engaged, with God, in the task of becoming the person he intended us to be. Or as Hans Küng (1978, p. 601) puts it very succinctly: 'Why should one be a Christian? ... In order to be truly human.'

PERSONHOOD

The vocation of the People of God called to personhood cannot be fulfilled in either individual or sectarian isolation. It is a vocation which, in its turn, must involve an invitation *to* others to discover their own truly human possibilities. This will take a wide diversity of tangible forms – offering a listening ear, giving sacrificially to good causes, working to provide human styles of management, seeking to create and sustain human cities, caring for the preservation of the planet, working for justice and peace locally and globally. Through these means of grace a called laity will be calling all people to deeper understanding of what it is to be human, and to a commitment to make personhood a reality for all.

But this is only one side of the coin. For God's calling of you and me to personhood is constantly conveyed to us *by* others, Christians and non-Christians alike. Lay vocation is not about our discovering some elixir of life which we then offer to others in a spirit of Lady Bountiful. It is about a shared journey in which we have to respond to God's call to personhood through our fellows, often (as in the stories of Christ) unexpected and unattractive fellows, as fully as God is calling them to respond to us. Lay vocation, the call to personhood, is thus an 'all-in' affair. We are called by and respond to God's presence in and through others, even our enemies, just as often as we call them and await their response.

The Kingdom is not divided. It is the same Kingdom beyond the walls of the church as within it. We should not, therefore, be disturbed that God's call to personhood can come to us through the 'secular' as often as the 'sacred'; that we can learn as much, if not more, about the meaning of being human from those of other faiths and none as we can from our fellow Christians.

This does not mean that personhood is on offer everywhere we turn. Because we are part of a fallen humanity, we shall constantly come up against dehumanizing forces and destructive principalities and powers. Here the Christian community has the immense privilege of the role model of Christ himself, fully divine yet fully human, to which to relate. But even so, as our risen Lord, he will be as present in the lonely crowd and amongst the poor and the marginalized as he is within the Scriptures and the church itself.

Lay vocation, then, is about a shared call and mutual response to person-hood, individually and communally. It is not primarily about communicating 'the faith', looking for conversions or building up the church, though all these things may be involved. Our vocation is to become a human race fully alive and, as Irenaeus once put it, thereby glorify God our Creator.

THE CALL OF THE ORDAINED MINISTRY

So where does the ordained ministry fit into the frame? We have exactly the same vocation – for we too are human beings made in God's image. Our call, like that of every Christian, is the call to personhood – maturity in Christ. We are not exempt from the journey – nor can we ignore God's call, through many not of the community of faith, to open our eyes to new horizons and new vistas.

If the call of the ordained is distinctive, it is only in that we have a special role in fostering and developing the personhood of the people of God, whose would-be holiness is simply another word for wholeness. Thus it is a dreadfully serious state of affairs if worship and pastoral care and Christian education (as CIPL's *Survey* indicated; Clark, 1993) do not enable the laity to be enriched and grow as persons. For where this development is not occurring, no Kingdom can come on earth as in heaven. So the rediscovery of the centrality of the vo-cation of the whole people of God for the sake of world as well as church is of paramount concern for every one of us.

Theology and the human city
Martin Stringer

We are all theologians ...

WHY DO WE NEED THEOLOGY?

... Theological reflection, and the active response to that reflection, are clearly two different parts of the same process. They are not identical. The Pastoral Cycle, and similar schemes for doing theology, stress a three-stage process: analysis of the situation, theological reflection, and active response. All three stages are necessary but each stage is distinct. The action cannot take place without first analysing the situation and secondly reflecting on that situation theologically, 'seeing' and 'judging' as the original Young Christian Workers motto put it. To embark on action without theological reflection, however, does not negate theology, it merely leaves it as implicit.

It was clear from my work in Manchester that everybody, local clergy, congregations, social activists, even dedicated non-churchgoers, had their own implicit theology, their own vague and unformed ideas of who God was and what relevance God had for their situation, of what it means to be human and how we are to relate to other human beings. These implicit theologies did not take long to discover. They were often crude, often contradictory, often misguided in the sense of containing a hidden sexism or racism, or a condemnatory attitude to other members of the community. As long as these theologies remained implicit, however, they were able to influence the action that was undertaken without themselves being called into question.

What becomes obvious, therefore, is that theology, far from being an optional, irrelevant, extra, is something that is central to the way in which all people responded to their situation. Some are willing to face up to their theology, and challenge it, while others prefer to marginalize it and so fail to face up to their own implicit assumptions and judgements.

WHO IS THE THEOLOGIAN?

We are all theologians ... We all have some ideas about God, about what it means to be human, and about how we should relate to other human beings. For most of us, however, these ideas remain unformed and unchallenged.

I spent many hours, whilst working with congregations in the inner urban areas of Manchester, listening to people talk about their theologies, either informally over coffee, or more formally in discussion groups. What struck me was the hidden depth and commitment, behind the crudeness and the often contradictory nature, of people's fundamental theological reflection. I was also struck by their lack of knowledge and understanding of the Christian tradition. Much of the discussion about local theologies assumes that with a bit of coaxing ordinary people can be encouraged to bring to the surface their implicit theologies and express them in terms of the tradition, and that this will be an 'authentic' theological tradition for that community.

The idea of local, authentic, theological traditions arising out of the struggles of people living within the city is an appealing one, but it is also one which we should treat with a great deal of caution. I have already noted that many implicit theologies are based on understandings which have no place in the Christian tradition, such as sexism or racism. If we were simply to build a local theology out of the implicit theologies of local people then it could easily be seriously flawed. We also have to acknowledge the desperate lack of knowledge about the wider Christian traditions within our society as a whole, and the same kinds of flaws in many of those traditions. Simply allowing people to construct their own theology in isolation would be a very dangerous activity.

However, obversely, simply allowing the theologians, those who have the opportunity to immerse themselves in the tradition, to dictate a theology to the people of the city would also be disastrous. The theologian is an important figure in any kind of theological discussion of the human city. We would not expect to enter into discussion about urban poverty, for example, without first listening both to those who suffer from such poverty and to those who have studied the causes and possible solutions to that poverty. For a fully rounded picture we need to listen to the people and to the 'experts'. The same should be true for theology. To get a fully rounded theology for the human city we need to be involved in a dialogue between those who are involved in the various aspects of the city and those who have, either through academic study or through prayer and contemplation, immersed themselves in the study of the Christian tradition. Only out of this dialogue can a possible theology emerge which could lead to effective action.

WHAT IS THEOLOGY?

. . .

If we start with the tradition then any, even cursory, glance at that tradition in its completeness will show that we have just under two thousand years of specifically Christian reflection and commitment to draw on. Clearly the biblical texts have a privileged position within this reflection, but Christian theology did not stop at the end of the first century. Christians have continued to live out their lives as Christians, to reflect on that life, to pray and to get involved in direct action. They have continued to write about that experience. We have that reflection, prayer, action and writing to draw on and we should rejoice in the diversity on offer.

Theology, however, is not simply tradition. Neither is theology simply an intellectual activity. If we go back to the Pastoral Cycle we see that the analysis comes first, the detailed study of the situation, the reflection on experience. Then comes the theology. This is expected to be something more than simply further reflection or discussion, and the word 'judge' from the Young Christian Workers probably makes this clearer than many other terms. The theological reflection is there to judge the situation, to make a decision about that situation from the position of commitment, to go beyond the human reflection to the Divine Word.

Christian theology is first and foremost a commitment to the God revealed to us in the life, death and resurrection of Jesus Christ. It is only from a position of faith in God that theology can be undertaken. It is for this reason that individuals who have immersed themselves in prayer are as much theologians as ones who have immersed themselves in the intellectual tradition. It is also, I would suggest, this commitment to God, this acceptance of dependence on God, that has been lacking in so many local and academic traditions of theology in recent years, and which makes them appear so irrelevant.

. . .

Martin Stringer is a Lecturer in Theology in the Department of Theology at the University of Birmingham.

The prophetic tradition in the contemporary world
John Davies

There are as many kinds of prophecy as there are prophets.

There are as many kinds of prophecy as there are prophets. Students of the Bible will know that there are dozens of different angles on prophecy which can be based on Scripture ... I will, therefore, limit this paper to four themes for which I think we need to watch out if we are to share in authentic prophetic tradition in our own day.

THE PROPHET IS CONSERVATIVE

The prophet is a conservative figure. I do not mean by this that the prophet subscribes to *The Daily Telegraph*. What is today often called 'conservatism' is not much more than the interest-group of those who happen to have done well out of the most recent phase of our history.

The genuine prophet stands for values which are in danger of being abolished by 'progressive' individuals who benefit from the way things have been going. For instance, on the one hand, the 'gospel' of apartheid was highly congenial to that minority of the South African population which was advantaged by racial segregation and job reservation: on the other hand, the church was behaving according to its most conservative traditions when it opposed the upstart novelty of institutionalized racism. When the church insisted that differences of ancestry and cultures should not be allowed to infringe the unity of the Body of Christ, it was claiming the central commitment of its ancient faith. So John the Baptist appears as an almost archaic figure, dressing himself recognizably in the uniform of a kind of person who had been obsolete for some hundreds of years. He accepts a diet consisting only of what could be gathered from the desert, without the interference of modern processes of manufacture and trade which were so tied up with the oppression of the peasant communities he was addressing.

The prophet represents God's intervention on behalf of those who get least advantage from things as they are. The prophet does not want to destroy government: it is the rich, not the poor, who resent being governed.

Prophets intervene to remind government of government's unfulfilled agenda, to remind the priests of the central purposes of God's will. They may look and sound old-fashioned; they do not move with the times, because the times are moving in the wrong direction. They may well be, in fact, elderly people, old enough to remember what conditions were like before certain institutions of justice and compassion were created; old enough, therefore, to want to safeguard them against policies which would weaken them and which would put health care and education, for instance, at the mercy of the forces of competition and private gain.

THE PROPHET IS AN AMATEUR

The prophet is not a paid or licensed agent of state or church. Amos is seen as a threat by the religious establishment and by the government. The church appeals to the state to get rid of him. Amaziah, the priest of Bethel, sees him as a subversive element who is bound to be in the pay of the enemy: so Amos should go back to those who provide him with his meal-tickets, and stop disturbing the peace by which the peasants are kept in order. Amos insists, in reply, that he is an uneducated peasant himself, and thus has no interest of his own to serve. (For several years, I was priest of a huge rural parish in the Eastern Transvaal, a bitter and cruel area based on a town called Bethal: I still wonder which was my actual model, Amaziah or Amos!)

So, can the prophet speak from inside the system, from a place within the establishment? It is, perhaps, easier to be the conspicuous outsider like Elijah than the conscientious minister of state like Elisha. There are those who speak as if the conversion of Constantine were the worst thing which ever happened to Christianity: it led to bishops wearing purple, and the church using the apparatus of the state to impose its will. It led to religious wars between Christians, in which the main difference between the two sides was that one preferred to behead the other side, whereas the other side preferred burning. But Constantine was also on the right side, as we would think, on issues such as capital punishment, child abuse, slavery and even 'keeping Sunday Special'. If the followers of Jesus get the opportunity to influence society in the direction of justice and compassion, should they not do so?

But, even if the prophet does become part of the establishment, he remains an amateur. Jesus makes it clear that there is not much hope for the lawyer so long as the lawyer argues about certain categories of humankind as identified by the establishment. But there is hope for him if he can recognize that it is the unqualified Samaritan who is, in practice, free to obey the law of compassion. Even the lawyer can have the freedom to be more than a lawyer, and behave like a Samaritan. There is just hope for the religious official, provided that in some things he remains an amateur.

But a reluctant amateur. Prophets find themselves compelled to take their stance, unwillingly. The greatest danger for the prophet is to become too adjusted to the role, to become a kind of regular prosecuting counsel. Once this happens, he finds himself positively wanting his adversaries to become more stupid and evil than they are so that he may gain status. Satan, as a figure in Scripture, starts off as prosecuting counsel, then becomes tempter, and ends up as arch-fiend. Self-appointed prophets, beware!

THE PROPHET IS INTO PUBLIC ISSUES

'The earth is the Lord's and all that is in it: the world and its people belong to the Lord.' This is the starting-point. The prophet is certainly a religious figure, not simply a political activist. Political activists, ancient and modern, have tended to see the world as a place of struggle between rival interest groups. This was the general assumption of the nations around Israel in Old Testament times: different gods, or Baalim, stood for the interests of different groups who had managed to establish tenure over the land and to control the wealth produced from the land.

Against this essentially idolatrous type of both theology and land-tenure, the prophetic tradition stood for the claim of the one true God upon all the land and its resources. Those who worship the one true God would put their worship into practice by recognizing the rights of all people to a share in the wealth produced from the land. So, for instance, the Sabbath law was not just a provision for people to be able to go to church without distraction: the Sabbath law ensured that, for one day in every seven, the economic distinction between employer, employee and unemployed would not apply: all classes were to have equal access to spiritual and social renewal.

The law of Moses was designed to prevent permanent accumulation of land and, therefore, of the power of one person to make another person a permanent debtor. It was not forbidding private ownership: nor was it preventing people from gaining wealth through their own hard work. But it would prevent the wealth produced by the whole community from being diverted into the pockets of those who had established ownership of land. In our day, land values can rise sharply with, for instance, the opening of a motorway. The value created by the corporate activity of the whole community is claimed by those who have the good luck to own land in the right place: whereas affordable housing ceases to be available for the basic creators of wealth, such as farm workers. It is not the cost of house-building that has made housing so expensive: it is the rise in land-values. The law which the prophets affirmed required that those who possessed land should pay a compensation to those who did not. Any claiming of the prophetic tradition for our contemporary world would have to include a critique of our systems of taxation and land-tenure: nothing, surely, could be more fundamentally public and basically ethical. And yet how often do you see these subjects addressed in our standard dictionaries of Christian ethics?

THE PROPHET LOOKS FORWARD WITH HOPE

In all these matters, the prophet is one who looks forward. The Holy Spirit spoke through the prophets – through those who were not yet naming the Son of God and not yet knowing the grace of the Gospel, but who could see something of the eventual hope that would be brought by Christ. For Christians, there is still the hope that Christ will come as the saving judge, to eradicate compassionlessness from the universe.

At the same time, the church has traditionally recognized prophets from cultures other than those of the Bible. We find a solidarity in yearning and a common language of hope: that is the prophetic attitude. We look forward to the

Christ who still has much coming to do and many arrivals to complete. The prophet who celebrates the past by both remembering and praising will have the ability both to wait for and to hasten the coming of the day of the Lord (2 Peter 3.12).

John Davies was formerly the Anglican Bishop of Shrewsbury.

The missionary structure of the congregation

The life of many congregations is at a low ebb. There is considerable confusion about how the church can ever again establish a lively and creative relationship with a 'secular' society. But if our calling as Christians is about the building of a Kingdom Community rooted in our personal and corporate flourishing as human beings, and if the most authentic way of initiating such a transformation is through genuine dialogue, then the missionary structure of the congregation has to reflect this new stance and culture.

Congregations of this kind will work to become true learning communities, deeply aware of their Christian identity, yet open to change in the light of the truth they discern in all creative organizational forms. To view the missionary congregation as a learning community will in turn have profound implications for the quality of its worship, its form of pastoral care, the nature of Christian education and, not least, the kind of support offered to church members as they pursue their common calling in daily life.

Engaging in mission – the church as a 'learning organization'

David Clark

The church's mission is to go on learning how best to transform itself and the world, of which it is an integral part, into the wholeness of the Kingdom Community.

Management rules – OK! Not for many years (indeed ever before?) have such utopian expectations been placed on the shoulders of 'management' to deliver the goods. 'Total quality assurance, development plans, outcome objectives, top-slicing, profile components, cost-benefit analysis, performance indicators' – are but fragments of the new language of salvation. Our temptation as Christians in public life is to write off such jargonese as the pursuit of false gods. But we must be careful, in the midst of this brave new world, not to throw the baby out with the bath water. For among all the gobbledygook are some newly minted concepts which may have a good deal more to teach us than at first sight meets the eye. One such is that of 'the learning organization'.

The 'learning organization' is one of those new concepts which seems to buck the trend. Much current in management-speak is about control and competition. The concept of the 'learning organization' is different. It describes the response of insightful management consultants to the fact that we now live in a constantly changing world in which flexibility and the sharing of resources are essential, not only for the survival of companies, but to enable them to grow and develop as dynamic entities. Such openness to change and challenge requires a whole new approach not just to the manufacturing process but to the use of human resources.

What is beginning to dawn on a once hierarchical and over-structured commercial and industrial sector should be food and drink for a church whose mission is pre-eminently that of helping to bring in the Kingdom. For such a mission is about transformation. Transformation means change and change means the ability of people to learn how to change. If, therefore, the church ceases to learn, ceases to be a learning organization, then not only will it become moribund as a human institution, but deny its mission as a transforming community of faith. But what does it mean for the church to be (or become again) a learning organization? For, as we know, it has for so long and in so many situations stopped learning.

BEING IN TOUCH

A learning church, like a learning company, must be in touch with the whole of life – the lesson of the incarnation. Because the church is primarily in the business of people – their transformation and fulfilment – it must above all be in touch with people. People in their homes and neighbourhoods of course – but also in their daily life and work in the great secular institutions of society. A church cannot learn how to change and transform society, let alone itself, if it is not continuously engaging, sharing and working together with the wider world in addressing fundamental questions of common concern. The church is not 'teacher' and the world 'learner' – we are all teachers and all learners in the business of life.

'Being in touch' means being in touch with the whole gamut of everyday life: what it feels like to be a lorry driver, a policeman, a cleaner, a miner, a greengrocer, an engineer, a banker, as well as a teacher, nurse or social worker. It means being in touch with people now – today in this 'modern' (or 'post-modern') urban, bureaucratic and mobile world of bewildering diversity and choice. It means learning how the Kingdom is being made manifest through new knowledge and new discoveries and how to discern its presence.

OWNING ITS MISSION

Although the learning organization is about new insights and transformation, it remains true to its mission as it sees it at any point in time. It is not for ever hedging its bets. So with the church. To be a learning organization does not mean sitting on the fence. It means advocacy of the truths which the church espouses and the outcomes it seeks. How else can others identify what is on offer? How else can others commend or criticize it? How else can the church learn how to be engaged in its mission purposefully and creatively?

TAKING STOCK

Owning its mission, however, does not mean the rigidity or routinization of those programmes and processes springing from it. The learning organization is always 'a reflective learner'. This means having time and space to take stock; it means research and open-ended investigation; it means active listening; it means appraisal and evaluation. It is here that the church as a learning organ-ization so often begins to falter. It mistakes the old, tired words and symbols for strength of purpose and relegates learning to the bottom of the agenda. So we find growth in the faith stuck at the level of childhood, 'truth' becoming entombed in clichés, and 'transformation' itself being transformed into the per-petuation of anachronistic traditions.

Taking stock, being genuine 'reflective practitioners', is the antithesis of all this. It requires advocacy of the Kingdom whilst at the same time actively seeking to discern more fully, in the light of the living faith of those past and present, that Kingdom's ever-changing and mysterious outworkings in the whole of human life, 'sacred' and 'secular', private and public. Taking stock continues throughout every phase of the learning process. It leads into but also permeates deeply all aspects of the learning organization.

BEING SURPRISED

Learning organizations are for ever being surprised, and welcome the fact. A church which is no longer surprised – through reflection on life as it really is and people as they really are – cannot learn, cannot change and cannot transform itself or the world.

Only those ready to face the creative 'mismatch' of inherited culture and contemporary culture, of tradition and experience, of the local and the cosmopolitan, of dogma and discovery can be surprised. If life and work cease to surprise us we cannot be transformed. The church as a learning organization has to welcome and treasure surprise, for in the end its 'products' – hope, love, forgiveness, faith – are constant surprises and constant triggers for learning, or they are nothing.

ASKING QUESTIONS

The one ultimate hallmark of the learning organization is its capacity to raise questions in the light of stock-taking and being surprised, fundamental questions of values and belief. Where the church avoids such questions it is setting nurture and instruction above mature growth. It is placing the transmission of the tradition above the transformation of society. It is placing teaching above learning. This is a strange choice of priorities for a body who follows a leader who was forever challenging the old ways of looking at things, telling stories with no 'answers', and enabling people to discover and own truth for themselves. If the church is to proclaim its message of transformation in a changing world, then it ceases to promote learning as a journey of discovery at the cost of its integrity, and ultimately of its survival, as a community of faith.

TAKING RISKS

Learning organizations take risks. There is little learning in a cocoon. There is no knowing without testing possible 'answers' to questions posed. It is not just the world of science which needs hypotheses, the church too requires hypotheses about life and living in today's world, and needs to put them to the test. This is true not only of questions about the church's internal life – such as whether the ordination of women is or is not a 'breakthrough' – but of its mission of transformation in the midst of the ethical complexities and moral dilemmas of day-to-day life.

Learning organizations know that risk-taking will never succeed if there is no affirmation, trust, support and forgiveness of those taking risks. If the church is to learn how to change itself and society, it must enable its members to take risks, make mistakes and still sustain them in their transforming vocation. The church, as the Easter story reminds us, should be above all the champion of creative failure. A church which watches its risk-takers from afar but learns nothing from their prophetic insights is not transformed and cannot transform others. The church as a learning organization needs, therefore, to learn from its 'marginal' men and women – in base communities, in justice and peace networks, in community work, in the women's movement, in inter-faith dialogue, but above all in the thick of public life. It is often those living on the margins who have the most to teach us.

TAKING ACTION

The learning organization does not expect the few to take risks on its behalf whilst it does nothing. It does not view its risk-takers as fulfilling its responsi-bility for change and transformation. It learns from them – it responds to them – and it seeks to change itself in the light which their pioneering discoveries throws on its own transforming mission.

The learning church thus enables individuals – within its own and the wider world – to become increasingly 'autonomous'. It transforms them from depen-dent to independent persons, able to take responsibility for their divine voca-tion of becoming whole human beings. The learning church realizes its mission by liberating people to find dignity, integrity and fulfilment as co-workers with God in the re-creation of his world.

The learning church likewise enables people within its own company and the wider world – to become increasingly 'ecumenical'. It leads people from de-pendence and independence towards interdependence, able to recognize that the salvation of each depends on the salvation of all. The church's mission is to go on learning how better to transform itself and the world, of which it is an integral part, into the wholeness of the Kingdom Community.

Ministry in the world – the role of the local church

Dick Wolff

(A synopsis of a report following a sabbatical in the USA in the autumn of 1992)

Maybe the primary gifts people have to bring with which to build the fellowship are the joys, frustrations, concerns and gospel insights they discover in the world.

It is important to say at the outset that nowhere during my visit to the United States was it said that Christians with a demanding ministry in the world should be relieved of ministry in the church. All Christians are called to 'build the Body of Christ' – but does ministry in the church only mean giving time to running the organization? Maybe the primary gifts people have to bring with which to build the fellowship are the joys, frustrations, concerns and gospel insights they discover in the world. Offered to God and transformed by the Holy Spirit within the fellowship these, surely, are the church's fundamental building blocks. Yet they are the 'stones' which, if the church has not consciously rejected, it has yet to find a way of accepting.

Two warnings: many people will have great difficulty understanding the concept of being called to 'minister in the world' – at first. It may take months before the 'penny drops' as to what this is about, and a different language may have to be found. Secondly, there is an ever-present danger of creating an élite band of lay Christians whose personalities enable them to stand up and speak articulately about themselves, or who are in caring, people-oriented professions that people can more readily see as 'Christian'. Such élitism, however unintended, is fatal to the process.

KEY OBJECTIVES

What sort of place is an 'empowering church'? One of my American interviewees summarized it succinctly:

- a place to discover your gifts;
- a place to discover and declare your personal call to ministry (in the home, community, workplace and/or church);
- a place of caring and trust;
- a place of accountability in relation to your call;
- a place of worship.

She believed strongly that these five 'functions' should characterize each different subgroup in the church. They cannot be separated out and located in different parts of the church's life. Another interviewee, recognizing that Christians when they gather have widely divergent life experience and language to speak about it, suggested three key ways in which small groups can work to develop a common language with which to talk about ministry, call, or vocation:

- work to develop listening skills;
- stretch one another primarily with questions;
- use training and development tools and techniques (e.g. personality-type indicator exercises) to understand better and affirm who we are, and are not.

'PRIMARY POINTS OF BELONGING'

It is probably true to say that churches are made up of subgroups rather than individuals. Most individuals are comfortable with church life because they are part of a smaller, closer unit, be it a Scout group, choir, fabric committee, family or simply a small circle of friends.

All the churches I visited in the States had appointed a 'task force' to work with each of their church committees, reshaping their agendas. These were being asked how, through the activity for which they were responsible, they were listening to people's daily experience, and working with them to enhance their sense of themselves as 'called people'. The point was made that 'structures need to be nourishing people as well as expecting something of them', meaning that church committees themselves need to move beyond being just a place to serve, towards incorporating all the five key objectives above.

But the point about the 'primary point of belonging' is that it is not just church committees that need to adopt those objects. Every subgroup, because it has caring and trust at its heart, needs to be honoured, supported and challenged to see itself as a 'primary point of belonging' and empowerment – a 'spiritual life-support group'. Clearly, this means that ordained clergy cannot be running around doing the 'empowering'. Every aspect of the church's life has to become 'empowering'.

THE SUNDAY GATHERING: COMMISSIONING AND 'EMPOWERMENT' SERVICES

My visit taught me that a stronger emphasis needs to be put on a single multi-purpose gathering of the whole community on Sunday. The agenda of people's daily lives can be handled, either by shortening the traditional worship service and having group work before or after, or extending it and making it more participative and fluid. If worship is to be built on the agenda of people's daily lives, a machinery must be set up to enable this to happen, because otherwise it will not. The traditional service order is an excellent framework. Worship should follow a regular and reassuring pattern and it should be clear who is responsible for leading it. Continuity of leadership week by week is essential, which in many churches necessitates a worship committee, not an ordained minister. The practice of delegating complete authority for worship leadership to an array of visiting preachers is unacceptable. Responsibility for directing public worship must not be interpreted as a licence to dominate its content. The prayer of intercession is a key opportunity to have a 'time of sharing concerns and celebrations' with as much time given to this as is necessary. Genuine participation does not mean participation only by the extrovert and articulate.

'Commissioning' of lay people to particular ministries in the world is fraught with dangers and contradictions. Far better is a 'service of empowerment' akin to a service for healing, preferably with laying-on of hands. (Ordained ministers who are not prepared to put themselves forward for such support probably have not grasped the concept.) Better still if those requesting such a prayer are in the midst of the congregation, not out in front, and if everyone in the congregation has a hand on the person in front (like spokes of a wheel). Three elements should be included in the prayer:

- a reference by name to those asking for 'empowerment' which spells out what ministry it is they seek support in, and maybe why;
- thanksgiving that those people's ministries are being exercised on behalf of the whole congregation, and each member of it;
- an empowerment prayer for all those participating (not just the few) in their own daily ministry.

ACCOUNTABILITY

The difference it makes, calling a job in the world a 'ministry', is that it explicitly connects it with 'church'. It introduces a note of mutual accountability, albeit voluntary. (Some people find this idea liberating, others threatening.) If this mutual accountability does not find some means of expression, it is probably a misuse of the word 'ministry'. Also, both partners have to accept and declare it as 'ministry': one party cannot by itself. It is not only about 'sending' people into the world, but just as much about enriching, enhancing and strengthening the Body of Christ. The church community can only 'own' and benefit from a lay person's ministry in the world if it knows what that ministry is.

SPIRITUALITY AND RENEWAL

At root, all this is about spirituality. For many of my interviewees, discovering that they were ministers was a conversion experience. This had been both a liberating discovery and a source of frustration and impatience – both of which are hallmarks of a spiritual renewal movement in its infancy. As such, however, it benefits from not yet having been claimed as the exclusive preserve of a particular theological tendency (as has happened to so many other genuine renewal movements). It is an openness which is precious, and needs maintaining.

Dick Wolff was formerly Executive Officer of Coventry and Warwickshire Mission in the World of Work. He now works as Mission Enabler to the Wessex Province of the United Reformed Church and minister in the Oxford Group of the United Reformed Churches.

Worship which frees and unites
Dick Wolff

I see the function of liturgy as being not so much to provide the people of God with oxygen, as to lift their heads above water so they can breathe for themselves – as individuals, as groups and as a united but diverse community.

Having spent nine years on the fringe of the church, struggling to bridge the gulf between the two worlds of 'daily life' and 'Christian faith', and largely failing, I am more than ever convinced that liturgy – in particular the main Sunday act of worship – is the key to success or failure. It is the central event of the Christian community. Church structures and church programmes feed into it and are fed by it. Worship can and should be a transforming event, in which the created is renewed by its Creator. The inability of much contemporary worship to engage with the agendas of its participants' lives, unlock the worship and 'stir up the gifts of God' within them is the main stumbling block to the church's mission.

Worship is how the church breathes – it has to happen week in, week out, in a steady rhythm. The challenge that faces us is to learn how to become a 'breathing' body of 'breathing' individuals. At present, if they are not gasping for breath, many congregations are 'snorkelling' – the whole community is trying to 'breathe' through the worship offered by only one or two people. Some asphyxiate in the process. There are, of course, 'resource books' for worship, and there are people who earn their living writing prayers for others to say. These have their uses, but cannot be a permanent substitute. They are like oxygen tanks, which only delay the moment when the community has to surface and breathe for itself. I see the function of liturgy as being not so much to provide the People of God with oxygen, as to lift their heads above water so they can breathe for themselves – as individuals, as groups and as a united but diverse community.

In worship, a diverse collection of individuals and groups seeks a unity in Christ not only amongst themselves but with the world Church and the whole of creation. In the past, that unity was sought in a liturgical uniformity (prescribed framework and, to a great extent, content also). It turned out to be a disaster – it fragmented the church. Good liturgy is grounded in what we have in common. This means being ultimately grounded in two things:

- God, in whom all things have their right relationship;
- the aspects of human experience that are common to all human beings, regardless of race, culture, etc ... the 'common denominator of what it is that makes us human'.

For this reason, 'special services' that focus only on the distinctive experiences of this or that group within the congregation do not address the fundamental issue.

It is important that if a congregation is to 'think globally', a 'discipline' from beyond itself be acknowledged. But it is important to establish what *principles* this discipline is intended to uphold. I suggest there are two:

- There are recognizable cross-references to the liturgy of the world-wide church and traditions of the past, and an embracing of the whole of the scriptural witness, so that it expresses the essential unity of God's People in space and in time.
- It reflects the concerns of the whole world, not just a part of it. In particular, concerns for justice, peace and the integrity of Creation under God.

Rules, frameworks and specified content of 'centrally defined liturgies' need to be no more than are absolutely necessary to ensure that these principles are honoured.

However, if liturgy is something 'received' by a congregation, it is also the people's work. Unless it can be turned into worship it remains an empty ritual. There is no point having a Rolls Royce of a liturgy if the vehicle people need to unlock their worship is a bicycle. (A bicycle, although more effort, may be more in touch with the outside world and more conducive to individual participation!) If, as the Orthodox writer George Khodr suggests, 'liturgy is the cosmos in the process of transformation', we need to recognize that the cosmos being transformed here is, in the first instance, the worldly systems, myths, values and engagements that are ingrained in the lives of these particular worshippers (with their ensuing alienation from the Kingdom of God). 'Think globally' we must, but we must also 'worship *locally*'. If liturgy unites, it should also set participants free by allowing them to express what is within them. It must bring to the surface the specific tensions and contradictions in their daily lives, and deal with them. Perhaps it will go on to help them to make connections between these personal experiences, the experiences of others, and the interpreted experience of the world-wide church, and in it to discover liberation and hope. As the World Council of Churches once expressed it: 'Jesus Christ Frees and Unites.'

. . .

The gradual move towards worship 'in the round' is very important. God's holiness is now located at the heart of the community, not beyond it. The faithful are able simultaneously to focus on God and on one another as equals. Participation does not require role reversal.

Other changes have taken place in our society which should be causing a re-think of the way our liturgies are prepared and celebrated:

- Societal fragmentation is vastly increased. People live in very different worlds. It is unrealistic to expect one person to articulate successfully in prayer or sermon the specific concerns of every member of a congregation. 'Gathering' into a meaningful united community is far harder to achieve and needs greater attention in worship. It cannot be assumed that what unlocks worship for one group will do so for another, or that what evoked worship in the past will do so in the present.
- Authority now works very differently. Long gone are the days when the ordained minister was the only one with an education. There is a free market in ideas operating: religions are coming back into fashion (loads of them, all equally 'valid'). Formality sends different messages, and can easily look and feel absurd and ridiculous.
- Ideas are expressed less in the form of reasoned dissertation and argument and more in symbol and soundbite. The art of consciously creating imagery has reached a high level of sophistication.

The time has come when a devolved local worship leadership – a partnership between 'lay' and ordained – is going to have to be trusted to construct local liturgies that are nonetheless 'global', which 'unite' as well as 'free' people. However, in order to do that they will have to understand the processes involved in creating living liturgy, and how to strike the difficult balance between liturgy that is locally appropriate, responsive and participatory, but nonetheless securely anchored in the Christian story and the practice of the whole contemporary church.

The gift 'professional' liturgists (of which I am emphatically not one) have to bring is that they understand the principles underneath liturgy – the psychological processes that comprise liturgy, the theology and the human needs that are addressed in the various movements of liturgy. What we want from them is not pre-written, 'off-the-peg' liturgies. We do not need the fruits of their skills – we need them to pass on the skills themselves ... As an illustration of the sort of work that is required, try looking at a typical liturgy, and asking how the different stages in the process might relate to people's daily/public/working life:

1.   *Gathering/welcoming*: an opportunity to remind each other of the various worlds within which people move during the week and perhaps catch up on each other's news.

2.   *Adoration/confession*: focusing on the 'God in the midst', regaining perspective, openly acknowledging the ways in which we are ensnared in systems and practices that deny the Kingdom of justice, peace and integrity in creation.

3.   *'Ministry of the Word'*: a mutual 'working out' of strategies for withdrawing co-operation from whatever denies the Kingdom with the help of the Scriptures. Waiting on God for words of judgement, challenge, hope, forgiveness, encouragement – perhaps on the lips of fellow-worshippers.

4.   *Intercession*: a time for mutual sharing of 'concerns and celebrations', for holding our worlds/the World up before God in love.

5.   *Communion*: allowing God in Christ to take and own all this – a moment of transformation in which new possibilities are celebrated.

6.   *Dismissal*: a time of commissioning, in which individuals or groups may make specific resolutions for action and seek the community's blessing and support in the name of God.

A spirituality for Christians in public life

Gerard Hughes

We do not have a choice between spiritualities, one for private, the other for public life. There is one Spirit, one spirituality, which has to inform both our private and our public life.

A 'SPIRITUALIZED' FAITH

In the Jesuit house, where I did my noviceship, there was an ancient pump organ and novices had to do the pumping. Near the pump handle there was a paper arrow fixed to a cord with a lead weight at the foot of it. When the pressure was correct, the arrow on the cord was either aligned with, or below, a fixed arrow painted on the side of the organ. If the movable arrow was above the painted one, that was a signal to pump harder. One hot summer evening, a sturdy novice, tiring at his task, thought that he could save his energy if he were to stop pumping and just hold the movable arrow in line with the fixed one. He pulled on the cord, which broke, and the organ sighed into silence.

This is an image of what has happened with our spirituality. It is as though we had stopped pumping and were trying to hold the movable arrow in place. Our spirituality has become an activity separated from everyday affairs, with no obvious connection with public life. Even in private life, God is confined to those activities we call 'spiritual'. To let him loose on everyday private and public life would cause chaos. Readers can imagine this for themselves by doing the following exercise.

THE CAT AMONGST THE PIGEONS?

Imagine a ring at your doorbell one evening. There on the doorstep is the Risen Jesus himself. What do you do, how do you receive him? Presumably, you are full of wonder, astonishment, delight, summon the household, and find yourself making ridiculous statements to the Lord of all creation like 'Do make yourself at home. Please stay with us. We are delighted to have you.' Imagine Jesus has accepted your invitation and it is now two weeks later. How is the domestic scene? Has he changed since Gospel days, or is he still bringing 'not peace but the sword, setting daughter against mother, daughter-in-law against mother-in-law, son against father', and what has been happening over family meals?

Taking you at your word, Jesus invites his friends to your home. What kind of friends did he have in the Gospels and what kind of people are turning up at your house now? What are the neighbours saying, and what's happening to the local property values?

You decide you must not keep Jesus all to yourself, so you take him down to the local church to give a talk to the congregation. His little talks in the synagogue caused consternation, and the congregation tried to throw him off a nearby cliff. St Jude's Parish Church has no hill nearby, but his talk has offended the congregation, caused uproar and the parish has lost its principal benefactors.

You return home with Jesus. You have trouble on your hands. What are you to do? You cannot throw out the Lord of all creation. So look around the house, find a suitable cupboard, clear it out and do it up, sparing no expense. Get a strong lock and put Jesus inside, locking the door behind him. Put flowers and a lamp in front, and each time you pass bow reverently and say a little prayer. You now have Jesus where you want him and he does not interfere any more.

GOD IN ALL THINGS

If what I have written seems exaggerated and unfair, reflect, for example, on our national attitude to defence. No political party dares to question our policy of nuclear deterrence, if it is to have any chance in elections. Most Christians and church leaders agree with this policy. We pray to Christ for peace, while supporting a policy of defence which includes the building of four Trident submarines, each submarine with a fire power equivalent to almost 5,000 Hiroshimas, the weapons constructed not for defence, but for first strike.

We need a spirituality both for private *and* for public life which acknowledges that God is in all things, that he is the God of the ordinary, always closer to us than we are to ourselves, and our relationship to him is in every decision we make in private *or* in public life. What determines our decisions? Is it love of wealth, possessions, power, status, prestige and honour for ourselves, or for our group or nation, or is it a desire to mirror in all our behaviour the justice, tenderness, compassion and gentleness of God?

We do not have a choice between spiritualities, one for private, the other for public life. There is one Spirit, one spirituality, which has to inform both our private *and* our public life.

Gerard Hughes SJ is deeply involved in the development of a spirituality for those active in public life, not least in the field of peace and justice. He is a well-known author.

Theological auditing

Peter Challen

Theological audits have changed patterns of individuals' work and teams' contributions in many places where faith is not readily accepted as having pertinence.

. . .

Theological auditing has three main characteristics as an exploratory tool; flexibility, expandability and an extensive range of application. It requires the drawing together of both pastoral and prophetic skills and sensitivities. It has these main characteristics as a means of 'doing theology' – assuming and then exploring a comprehensive field of being Christ-like in ordinary tasks, undertaking a fresh exploration today of the Gospel that resonates through the biblical stories, with a foundation in the conviction that God reigns in every corner of our occupations.

. . .

Example: A Health and Safety Officer identified by a theological audit the disturbing sense of being forced to be a regulator for the Government. Her re-evaluated discipleship within her professional capacity led to recognition of the need to be an enabler for the intrinsic worth of health and safety in each place to which she went. It gave her courage to leave the relative security of the civil service and painfully to earn the authentic status of an independent consultant. After two years in the wilderness her consultancy now flourishes; and levels of health and safety rise significantly.

. . .

Example: Twenty persons each year, in training for ordination to stipendiary or non-stipendiary ministry, submit themselves to a theological audit in the third year with painful but exhilarating effect. For many this is the first time they have ever been asked to turn the implications of faith towards their own occupation in 'secular' setting. A 1992 audit carries this postscript: 'This has been an exciting and immensely valuable piece of work. I found it very difficult to do, particularly at the beginning. The original brief described it as possibly daunting. It was, but I feel that I have grown with it and it with me, sometimes very slowly, sometimes at sprintlike pace. At times I have been astounded by the thoughts that working on this has generated and the areas that it has drawn together, into some form of wonderful tapestry. It has radically affected my thinking about my work and about those with whom I share it. It has brought many areas of biblical foundation into sharp local focus. I have been enabled and encouraged to develop a tool which will allow me to assess my work and ministry and in a way I did not think possible.'

. . .

The auditing pattern is simple; the execution demanding. There are four stages.

1. Themes of faith, as they represent its comprehensive, contemporary and everywhere pertinent nature, are explored. Then the neglected themes (usually those with corporate and global implications beyond the simply intimate) are identified and examined. Trust between auditor and voluntary client is a requisite. That trust must grow in these preliminary efforts to identify neglected themes of our biblical faith.
2. Only when and if trust between auditor and the person audited does grow can they then look to see if some themes (one hopes the tougher ones) are affirmed at work, and acknowledged openly where they are affirmed already. Themes such as these at first perplex but soon stir to intriguing new aspects of discipleship: Creation (ecology), Heritage (wisdom and gift); Jubilee (regular restructuring for justice), Shalom (an all-pervading peace with justice), Covenant (contrast with contract in our present culture). The bequest to be recovered stretches on and on as the audit helps our search.
3. Next we look for blocks that frustrate the interpretation and application of those themes.
4. Finally, we devise, and hold to, step-by-step ways that avoid or overcome the blocks. This lets higher responsibilities come into play, bringing justice, peace and the sustaining of the integrity of creation to bear upon a decision, an action or some aspect of the corporate plan.

Theological audits have changed patterns of individuals' work and teams' contributions in many places where faith is not readily accepted as having pertinence: in accounting and auditing, in contracts and covenants, in perceptions of wealth, in training, in redeploying, in brokerage, in information technology, in restructuring, even in banking and so on, and so forth . . .

Everyday ethics: where do we begin?

Richard Jones

There are ... three fundamental ways of 'doing ethics'.

...

In the Old Testament, and carried forward into the New, there are set out three fundamental ways of 'doing ethics'. We need to practise all three alongside each other.

'DOING ETHICS' – THE BIBLICAL WAY

1. Let us heed wisdom

The 'Wisdom literature' has an honoured place in the Old Testament, although little Christian preaching or teaching refers to it. It advocates that one discerns what is right, by noting what works best in this world. For example, respect for one's elders works very well, according to the teaching. Refusal to be bewitched by alluring women – good advice for young men. Live in serenity, and do not get frantic. Do not set your heart on high and impossible objectives. Care about the poor. Promote justice. These practices actually work well.

That may sound like a form of moral philosophy which appeals peculiarly to the English – utilitarianism. Do what is likely to produce the most happiness. But it is actually much more profound, because the heart of 'wisdom' is in living close to God and trying to see life as he does – that is, from the great big perspectives of the God who runs the whole universe. Furthermore, the New Testament tells us that Jesus comes amongst us as the supreme Wisdom of God. So 'heeding wisdom' is far, far more than enlightened common sense or shrewd observation; it is trying to see life as God in Christ does.

2. Let us heed laws or rules

Ask the average Christian how one knows what God requires, and the reply is: the Ten Commandments. They are deeply etched into our moral awareness, which is fine. But most of them are negative, telling us what not to do. Do not commit adultery ... That is good advice, but it does not tell us how to promote a happy marriage. The commandments offer a type of hedge, keeping out many unworthy activities; fairly helpful, but not helpful enough. And further, they tell us little about the right motives for our actions, save that we must not covet. We all know that our motives matter; if they are twisted or corrupt, so will be our decisions.

Nonetheless, rules, laws, commandments; all are useful. We should observe them. It is noticeable that most professions today have 'Codes of Conduct', ground rules which offer guidance. Many of these codes have been distilled from years and years of experience, and merit honour. Similarly, nations look to observe the International Declaration of Human Rights which offers principles which all civilized people should respect. So does the law of the land. One should assume that if one proposes to act in a manner contrary to the law, or the Declaration, or codes of conduct, then one is likely to be wrong.

And yet, and yet … All codes and commandments remain conservative, restrictive and, as already noted, unable to help form the motivation for doing the right. One can often keep the law from the desire not to get into trouble, not to do anything out of the ordinary, to play safe. So law cannot be the last word – nor is it in the Bible.

3. Let us heed the word of prophecy

God, says the prophet, demands a radical, risky and almost absurd respect for the mighty principles of justice and mercy. You can almost forget everything else! But you cannot forget the claims of the poor and weak, the widow and the downtrodden, the stranger in the gate. Nor can you forget the claims of the good earth and the beasts, the seas and the creatures that swarm there. They are all God's and God loves them. They all have rights, and far more than rights. They have inherent value, bestowed by God through an extravagant love that demands justice all round.

Yes, and mercy. Mercy is not a weakness, but the ultimate in strength. Mercy forgives and is forgiving. It allows individuals and communities to make fresh starts, cancels debts and holds out hope. It is essentially creative, building up what is cast down, binding together again what was torn apart and divided. It is sacrificial, a way of giving out and spending and sharing. What does the Lord require of you, but to do justice, show mercy, and walk humbly with your God? And is not Jesus the Prophet supreme? Is not his way of love the ultimate demonstration of justice-rich mercy? Be like him. Have the mind that was in Christ.

Richard Jones was Chairman of the East Anglia District of the Methodist Church, a former President of the Methodist Conference, and is Editor of *The Epworth Review.*

The local church at work – triggers for awareness-raising

Gill College

How can the work life and church life of Christians be more effectively related?

How can the work life and church life of Christians be more effectively related? We are quite good at being able to state the problem that work and church life are not related, but not very good at seeing how this might be. The following are suggestions that might be the first stage of awareness-raising in the local church about the world of work ...

THE WORLD OF WORK IN WORSHIP

A person in a particular type of work is asked to write a prayer for the congregation to use about her work. A completely free hand is given. It can be any type of prayer. It is distributed to the congregation as they come into church. During the service the person is asked to talk about their work for five minutes – they then lead the congregation in the prayer. The congregation is asked to use the prayer in church meetings and in their private devotions during the next month. The following month another person does the same thing. Different categories of work could be presented each month. In a year, a congregation would have been made aware of a dozen types of work and the type of prayers that are needed for those situations.

People may be shy to talk for long about work in a church service. One way to encourage this would be for the preacher to interview two or three people about what they will be doing at 10 a.m. on Monday morning, and the intercessions then designed around what people say.

Local preachers and lay readers could be encouraged to use work-related issues in sermons. All people conducting services could be encouraged to pray specifically for people in routine work situations, not just at times of crisis. A thematic approach might help hold different work together, e.g. selling or moving house might include the building industry, house agents, solicitors, removal people, gas, electricians, telephone company workers.

'What is work' could be a theme for a family service. Placards with activities like playing, sewing, reading, mending a car, working in a factory, taking a photo, gardening, washing-up, could be held up by children. The leader of the service asks which people are working. Which is a leisure activity, which another boring job to be done? Who gets paid? End the discussion by saying: 'There are three types of work: creative, sustaining and repairing. They are three types of work God does. He does not get paid but asks us to work with him.' This could be followed by a sermon exploring how we share with God in these three types of work. This places daily work in God's orbit.

Consider preparing an annual service of re-dedication for people in their work place. (For Methodists this might be included within the annual Covenant Service.) At the same time include unemployed and retired people in the congregation. This acts as a standing in solidarity with them. Initiatives between people in paid employment, the unemployed and retired might start taking place. Prepare a commissioning service for people beginning work. This could be for school leavers, graduates and those starting new jobs ... A house group could be invited to produce ideas for meditation around the theme of work, either paid or voluntary, for each day of a week: a simple outline of the work concerned; verse of Scripture; a thought; an action; a prayer. A service could be created using these ideas. The congregation could be given these meditations and invited to use them the following week.

WORK ON THE MAP

Along with these ideas a large-scale local map could be produced. People could be invited to put on it a flag of where they work and the type of work they do. Retired people could be invited to place where they live, what they are retired from and any voluntary work they do. Unemployed people could be invited to do the same thing. The employment office, job centre, and other benefit offices and post offices where benefits are paid out could be flagged. Schools could be flagged where children go to work. If people work a distance from the locality, people's names could be on a road or railway station and the name of the town mentioned. This would be an exercise that puts work into the context of the community. It also recognizes the idea that work is not just paid employment. It could be called 'The dispersed church'. It would be a visual presentation that could be followed by ideas in a sermon about us each being representatives of the body of Christ from that church in the work place.

WORK REPRESENTED VISUALLY IN CHURCH

Look around the church – are there any symbols or images that speak of God in everyday ministry? Make a banner to illustrate being a Christian in daily work. A simple idea is to have a table in an obvious place as people come in or go out of church. Someone is responsible for each week placing on it a visual representation of a type of work or an item used by a person at work. Names of people who are in that type of work could be on the table and these names read out in the intercessions. People could be invited to add their name to the list if they did not appear on it. The object could be carried forward, with the offering, by a person doing the type of work represented.

Plan an all-age activity to make a collage of everyday work as an opportunity to serve God. If a geographical area had work of a particular type, this could be represented. If the work were of an artistic type, a piece made by a person could be displayed in the church. Ask two adults and two children to lead prayers of intercession while the congregation look at the collage.

SHARED WORK STORIES

In large churches people could be given the opportunity of meeting others in related fields – even if only occasionally – to learn about concerns and discuss ethical issues.

Church newsletters and magazines could carry stories and prayers about members' working concerns. A suburban church and rural church could exchange work stories.

Each church could designate one person to develop an awareness of lay ministry in the members' work life amongst the congregation. A noticeboard could be created to keep items of work news in the forefront of the congregation's mind.

. . .

Gill College trained as a nurse and midwife and has worked with indigenous people in Peru, as a lay worker in Birmingham City Centre in pastoral and in outreach ministry with homeless young people. She is now a Methodist minister working in Panama.

The missionary structure of the institution

Just as a new kind of ministry to the public arena will require a new kind of missionary congregation, so it will necessitate a new form of missionary institution. What the latter will look like will only emerge over time, but some markers are already beginning to be put down.

The new missionary institution will provide a sustainable framework for equipping its members to fulfil their calling in the public arena. Preparation for lay ministry in the world will depend on skilled facilitators working with groups and networks, many of these sector related, in an ongoing learning process. Lay appraisal with an emphasis on the whole person and the whole of society will be on offer alongside clergy appraisal.

The nature of the ordained ministry in such an institution will be of crucial importance. It will involve the development of a new role within congregational life more fully directed to those working in the public arena. This role will be shaped in part by current modes of chaplaincy or non-stipendiary ministry. But the future missionary institution will require innovative forms of ordained ministry, a situation which will have radical implications for clergy training.

A future missionary institution will also need styles of leadership very different from those which exist at present. These will be shaped by developing forms of secular management (which in fact often derive their core principles from Christian values). Leadership of this kind will be far more about crossing 'the great divide' between the sacred and secular, than about the maintenance of the institutional church as such.

The Portsmouth Faith and Work Project – raising questions

Ann Leonard

Joy in the discovery of the power of telling our own stories ...

In 1992, I was appointed by South Hampshire Industrial Mission (SHIM) to run a two-year Faith and Work Project in the Portsmouth area...

INITIAL RESPONSES

Many Christian people I meet are searching for a way of integrating the currently separated aspects of their lives and wish to have some forum for voicing their frustrations with the split between the expression of faith in worship on Sundays, and the living of life on Monday through to Saturday. These people expressed a longing for teaching, especially through sermons, and a chance to be supported and enabled to grapple theologically with the issues that they are facing every day. Where I have been given the opportunity by ministers to invite people to come together to explore faith and work issues, this 'theological grappling' has developed quite naturally. For many it has brought their faith alive and given them a new enthusiasm both for their work and their worship – a form of spiritual renewal – which they had not thought possible.

It has also led, in some cases, to the expression of a healthy disillusion and dissatisfaction with our main liturgical diet and a wish to be enabled to offer the whole of life at the Eucharist, that is the reality of how we spend our time each day, whether in tedious and monotonous activity, in stressful, high pressured work, or in making difficult managerial decisions (such as making people redundant or coping with the fear and reality of redundancy).

WORKING FROM EXPERIENCE

Through using the raw material of the members' own working-life experience, past and present, and the ensuing theological reflection on it, the groups have become vehicles for support, nurture, spiritual 'stock-taking' and theological audit (in the way Peter Challen speaks of it). I have frequently been surprised and delighted at the level of trust that has built up in the groups with whom I have been working – and the level of honesty and vulnerability that has been risked and accepted.

The feelings expressed have included:

- *Relief* at being able to voice fears, anxieties, doubt, pain and anger, and at its being understood and accepted; relief at realizing that one is not alone – that others have similar stresses and anxieties;
- *Delight* in the spin-offs from this task-orientated group-work – including getting to know fellow church members at a deeper level, feeling listened to and thus valued as a person; delight at coming across different strategies for coping that others have found helpful, and joy in the discovery of the power of telling our own stories – a form of witnessing and the best type of evangelism that I have yet encountered!
- *Shared frustration and dissatisfaction* with 'the Church'. In many cases this has led from a feeling of impotence, through solidarity to hope, and then to an increase in self-esteem as the possibility for change has been acknowledged, and even achieved in some cases.
- *A wish to share this 'good experience'* (good news?) with others so that more faith and work groups can grow out of the original one. This, when it happens, is an excellent cellular and dynamic way forward – which guards against groups becoming inward looking and 'static'.

. . .

The fundamental question that each participant tried to answer was ... How do I recognize and relate to God in the part of my life that I call work? Many other questions arose from the attempts to answer this initial one and each one of them would make an ideal topic for a sermon, or discussion groups, in its own right.

. . .

Ann Leonard is a trained counsellor and formerly worked with South Hampshire Industrial Mission (SHIM) as Project Officer for the Portsmouth Faith and Work Project. She is now an Anglican priest serving as curate in the parish of Farlington, Portsmouth, and Assistant to the Rural Dean.

Faith and work Guildford-style

David Welbourn

What really matters is a depth of penetration that will ensure lasting results.

The programme described here ... began in summer 1992 with a letter from the Bishop of Guildford to the rural deans and lay chairmen/women of the twelve deaneries which make up the diocese. In his letter the bishop referred to the need to make connections between faith and work, and announced his personal support for a programme devised by the Surrey and NE Hants Industrial Mission and which was ready to be operated within the deaneries, taking two deaneries at a time.

...

LESSONS LEARNT

Experience in operating the programme with the first two deaneries highlighted both strengths and weaknesses. The support of the bishop was fundamental but so was the co-operation of the rural deans and other clergy. The first seminar achieved a remarkable 95 per cent attendance rate. Weaknesses had been mainly presentational. For example, the parish proforma (a means of auditing the parish's response to its members' ministry in daily life) had been resented by some as bureaucratic and intrusive. One of the talks seemed suitable only for 'high-flyers' and some reckoned there had been too much 'talking *at*' people. These and other faults have been largely rectified in subsequent seminars.

About half of those present at the first seminar came to the follow-up seminar, and of those all but one accepted an ongoing role for themselves as world of work representatives. Subsequent meetings in the deaneries were requested. One follow-up idea that received wide support was an act of worship in Guildford Cathedral, which all those who had been through seminars up to the time of that service (including non-Anglicans) would be invited to attend.

An issue over which considerable early debate took place among the organizers was whether this programme should be denominational or ecumenical. We eventually decided that it should be both – denominational in that the programme should be run using denominational structures; but ecumenical in that the programmes would be offered to all the mainline churches.

...

What success may be claimed for these programmes? In terms of denominational and geographical spread, and in terms of the enthusiasm of those who have participated, results have so far been quite encouraging. But what really matters is a depth of penetration that will ensure lasting results. Our ultimate hope is that all the churches in all the mainstream denominations will be seen to be taking the subject of faith and work seriously, and to be providing effective support for those members of their congregation whose main form of Christian witness and service is their workplace ministry. Whether, by God's grace, that goal will be achieved, only time will tell.

David Welbourn is Churches' Officer in Industry and Commerce with the Surrey and NE Hants Industrial Mission and Hon. Editor of *ICF Quarterly Papers* (the journal of the Industry Churches Forum, formerly Industrial Christian Fellowship).

Faith and work consultations in the Diocese of Rochester

Garth Norman and Gordon Oliver

... a number of sector-based 'faith and work' consultations.

Between 1988 and 1995 we organized a number of sector-based 'faith and work' consultations. These brought together people involved in a particular field of work, from senior managers to junior staff and volunteers, to consult upon selected issues of concern about how they live out their faith in their working lives. Sectors involved so far have been the law, health care, transport, retail selling, finance, manufacturing, public service, and the Channel Tunnel. The diocese organized and funded an initial meeting in each case, normally on a Saturday from 10 a.m. to 4 p.m. Participants who wished to do so were then encouraged to form a group to take responsibility for arranging further meetings with administrative support from the Director of Training.

The 'consultation' model proved popular, and in principle can be applied to any sector of faith and work activity. We recognized that a diocesan consultation may be a daunting experience for some people and began to consider the possibility of encouring more local, deanery or parish-based ways of promoting the aims of 'faith and work'. We found that our original approach of recruiting participants (by the bishop asking incumbents to nominate people to receive an invitation from him) became less effective each time it was used. Continuing to involve the bishop, but using PCC secretaries as our contact point, proved more productive.

Key to the success of a consultation is the co-opted member brought into the planning group to help set up an initial consultation in a sector. It is important to find someone who knows the sector and key people in it, and who also has the ability and enthusiasm to involve others in continuing the life of the 'sector group'.

By mid-1995 it was clear that the faith and work consultation process was coming to the end of this phase of its life in the diocese. Networks and contact lists were in need of renewing, a number of new staff in the diocese were still finding their feet, and the availability of key players to put their energy into these events was increasingly problematic. We therefore decided to discontinue the consultations for a time, but remain convinced of the importance of their contribution to increased awareness of crucial faith and work issues among the people of the diocese, and hopeful that after a break we may be able to find new openings to begin them again.

Garth Norman was Director of Training and is now Archdeacon of Bromley in the Anglican Diocese of Rochester.
Gordon Oliver is Dirctor of Training in the Diocese.

Resource groups – a project
Rachel Jenkins

... a self-help resource group ...

The project described below was undertaken from February to October 1990. It was an attempt to offer a self-help resource group to Christians experiencing a mismatch between the values characterizing their faith and those prevalent at work, and the tensions and frustrations resulting...

For this project we chose to have a group of people from mixed denominational backgrounds and working in the private, public and voluntary sectors. The mixture of working backgrounds is particularly important because it gives a broad outlook and understanding to the group. People from one occupation can often see openings and share successes from their own experience which might otherwise go unnoticed by people from other occupational groups.

The publicity invited people to participate who saw themselves in a cleft stick, struggling between insisting on their own values and losing their jobs, or doing what was expected and losing their self respect. Other choices outlined were staying quiet out of loyalty to their organization or speaking up and making themselves and others vulnerable; and following the values of their professional association or those of their employer. Leaflets about the project were distributed via church networks, and were enclosed with a periodical published locally. An article was also circulated to the national religious newspapers, some of whom published it. Selection for the group depended on whether people were free on the dates already fixed and whether, after an initial discussion, they felt at home with the philosophy of the proposed programme.

Through the publicity and initial contacts we knew that the participants came with a strong sense of commitment to their espoused values although these were not necessarily clearly articulated. They came with a noticeable degree of concern about the organization within which they worked and were people who were engaged in the struggle to relate their faith to their daily lives. Participants had different interpersonal and managerial skills.

. . .

PROCESS OUTLINE

Group members arrive with

- a strong sense of commitment to their values sometimes accompanied by a lack of clarity;
- uneasiness about their work or the organization where they work;
- rich experiences of struggling to make sense of their faith in the world;
- a mixture (including a lack) of skills;
- difficult questions;
- sometimes life-changing decisions to be made.

In the group

- they build trust with one another;
- which enables them to seek clarity about their own values (their origin, their ambiguity, their validity).

On the basis of this

- they analyse their own situation using appropriate tools (e.g. critical incident theory; organizational culture);
- they discover through analysis and reflection an understanding of their own strengths and weaknesses,
- the situation of others with similar views and the extent of their own influence.

All this leads

- to a greater confidence in what they can achieve, and enables them to make strategic plans.

THEOLOGICAL ISSUES

During the meetings, two questions emerged which are of great importance. The first is concerned with the development of a spirituality which makes an impact on structures. We were conscious of the individual form of much Western spirituality which spoke powerfully about personal conduct, but which virtually ignored the patterns of power which could promote injustice as well as justice; pollution as well as health.

The second question recognized the position of apparent powerlessness in which many people find themselves. We identified the need to develop a spirit of 'unquiet endurance', a kind of waiting, but not in a passive way as in Vanstone's writing (1982). We were aware that many people continue to be mentally and physically active, but are hedged about with organizational restrictions which make them powerless, but not passive, in significant areas of policy making.

. . .

Rachel Jenkins was the Mark Gibbs Fellow based at the William Temple Foundation, Manchester. She has worked for many years in adult and continuing education. Her current work is as tutor responsible for full-time college-based students at the Northern Baptist College, Manchester where she is teaching in the area of Church and Society.

Faith, lifestyle and membership of the Christian church
A framework for self-appraisal
Sue Clark

For Christians, the insights and concepts of faith serve to enrich a sense of wholeness and integration, to the extent to which we are able to bring them to bear on every aspect of our lives.

In parallel with the introduction of formal appraisal systems into the world of work, a number of Christian denominations, such as the Anglican and Methodist Churches, have produced frameworks for the appraisal of their ordained ministers. The original draft of what follows was written for the Birmingham District of the Methodist Church in an attempt to complement such materials with a framework which might prove helpful to laity.

The intention of what follows is to offer questions which lay people might find helpful in reviewing their own faith, lifestyle and church membership. It seeks to do this within a framework which takes as its starting point an acknowledgement that God's gift of an individual human life is the gift of a seamless whole. If, therefore, we want to appraise what we are personally making of this gift, we need to ask ourselves questions which will prompt us to bring together the differing contexts, experiences and learning of our daily lives into an integrated whole. For Christians, the insights and concepts of faith serve to enrich this sense of wholeness and integration, to the extent to which we are able to bring them to bear on every aspect of our lives. The following framework is one tool which may help with this process.

In order to give some overall coherence and structure to the questions as well as to reflect the Christian context of the framework, five linking concepts have been used as section headings. The concepts have been drawn from Avery Dulles' book *Models of the Church* (1974). They are: church as ... Sacrament, Community, Herald, Servant and Institution. If the church truly resides in its people, lay and ordained, and not in some falsely reified and separated 'establishment', then our lives in their wholeness are the real manifestations of the church of Christ.

1. Faith, lifestyle and the church as sacrament: Spirituality

What aspects of myself am I learning to value and to nurture?
What aspects of myself might I learn to view more creatively?

How can I better nurture my own emotional needs?

What might help me to deepen a sense of hope and purpose in life?

How can I increasingly experience a sense of renewal and recreation?

How can I find a sense of personal wholeness and integrity, especially when life brings experiences of pain or suffering?

Do I live with any concerns or worries which preoccupy me more than I would wish? For example:

- money and/or possessions
- health
- personal ambition
- other?

How can my present understanding of my faith help both myself and others to become better human beings?

How can I more meaningfully pursue my personal exploration of Christian faith? For example:

- where and when do I best pray/reflect?
- what books have I read recently that have proved helpful? In what way?
- am I making good use of available Christian literature?
- what helps me to worship?

Am I able to discern and foster a sense of personal vocation?

2. Faith, lifestyle and the church as community: Relationships

With whom could I more fully share the personal journey, questions and discoveries of my life?

How better can I discern and nurture the unique value of others?

Are there particular relationships in my life which make me anxious or which I find particularly hard to handle? If so, what can I do to improve them?

How can I bring about peace and reconciliation where there is injury, offence or hurt?

Do I find enough time to enjoy the company of those with whom I have close personal relationships? If not, what can I do about this?

To what extent, in my relationships at all levels, do I offer open and honest communication and true listening?

To what extent have I been able to find a group of people with whom I can worship meaningfully?

How can I contribute to a greater sense of community amongst those with whom I share important aspects of my life? For example, at home, at work, at church.

3. Faith, lifestyle and the church as herald: Mission

In what ways do I communicate to those I meet that I value them as equal and irreplaceable human beings?

How might I better communicate my beliefs and values to those I meet on a daily basis, so that they 'know where I'm coming from'?

How can I act and speak in a way that is more consistent with my beliefs and values in situations where others hold different views?

How can I more genuinely communicate my Christian values through the way I use my time, money and talents?

How can I keep myself well informed and politically aware about the wider world?

What opportunities do I take to promote peace and to redress injustice at any level? For example:

- in my neighbourhood or city
- in my workplace
- at a national or world level?

4. Faith, lifestyle and the church as servant: Stewardship

Do I take adequate care of my own physical health?

How do I use my material goods in a way that is not wasteful? For example:

- money
- house
- possessions?

How can I better share my resources with others?

Where and how can I use my time and talents in a way that enhances life for other people?

What opportunities have presented themselves recently where I have succeeded or failed in being of service to others?

How can I, in my lifestyle, try to be a 'friend to the Earth'?

Who can help me to review the work I do so that I can enhance its value for others?

5. Faith, lifestyle and the church as institution: Membership

Do I contribute enough time and money to maintaining the life of the institutional church?

In what ways could I more fully contribute my own particular talents and skills to enhance the church's life?

How can I help to develop within the church better ways of learning and new understandings of the Christian faith?

How could I better present the implications of my own new understandings for the church as an institution?

How could I more effectively participate in reviewing and, if necessary challenging, the institutional life of the church in the light of my developing understanding of the Christian faith?

Sue Clark works as an educational psychologist for a large West Midlands local authority. She is a Methodist.

Industrial Mission – future perspectives
Rowland Goodwin

Industrial Mission has been one of the most sustained, significant and creative ecumenical enterprises in Britain since the Second World War.

Modern Industrial Mission, with its teams of lay and ordained staff accountable to management/advisory committees and ecumenical councils, part model for Churches Acting Together, is barely three decades old. In that time Industrial Mission (IM) has done enough to put support for Christians, and others, at work securely on church agendas. It has shown real concern for key economic and industrial issues and the struggle by people for justice and survival in employment and outside it. It has broadened from its original chaplaincy base. It has developed collaborative links with a wide range of organizations. It has learned the importance of standing with those who have become the tragic victims of the biggest social upheaval since the start of the Industrial Revolution.

The dedication and hard work of full-time men and women is a sign of its commitment. They have developed a remarkable expertise in industrial relations, group dynamics, the economic development process, stress, marginalized working, school/industry links, transport, retailing, redundancy, working with the unemployed, linking faith and work, Europe, transnational organizations ... When most people at work are inhibited in some way about being entirely open and honest about company affairs, missioners have exercised both a prophetic and pastoral ministry.

A MAIN SOURCE OF CHURCH INTEREST

...

More than most sections of the church, outside the theological colleges, IM has taken theology seriously, both in wrestling to do it and apply it, and has worked hard at the development of more meaningful forms of worship. Without doubt it has been one of the most sustained, significant and creative ecumenical enterprises in Britain since the Second World War. In that sense the church, through thirty years of IM work, is better equipped for the economic and social challenges of the future than it was in the heady days of the 1950s. But I do not believe that the church as a whole is any less alienated from the world of work and the growing ranks of the unemployed. Nor do I think lay Christians feel more affirmed and supported in their secular employment by the church, particularly at neighbourhood level.

THE CHURCH AND CHRONIC SOCIAL DIS-EASE

The failure to win support for IM and what it stands for from among the mass of clergy and ministers, theological college tutors and congregations fills me with immense disappointment. As a committed IM person I have to say that we are not entirely to blame. I believe that the integrity of the church was dealt a devastating blow by its failure to find a way to unite for mission in the 1960s, 1970s and 1980s. Where IM was among those leading the way, the denominations refused to follow.

Committed IM persons, lay and ordained, know just how much industry and commerce have changed in those years. Many Christians have abandoned teaching, banking and the Health Service and 'got out' of industry and local government because they have not been able to tolerate the dehumanizing changes that have taken place. Others struggle on as best they can because they have no alternative. Attitudes to work have altered radically in the 27 years I have been a full-time industrial missioner. The growth of stress in work and an under-class outside it are but two disturbing signs of contemporary chronic personal and social dis-ease. IM has striven, and is still striving, to respond to these acute needs; attempting to address the immediate human problems and the deeper economic, organizational, political, ideological and spiritual issues that are their cause. This is where IM believes God calls the church to action. Where IM is able to work in a positive, professional, caring and creative way many secular agencies are only too glad to open their doors. But, as our friends who have been ordained to be Ministers in Secular Employment also say, it has often been extremely difficult to persuade the church that the world offers any kind of authentic opportunity for ministry other than evangelism.

Everything now hinges on what the churches, the main financial resource for IM, choose as priorities. There is still chronic division, but there are signs of a slow stirring towards more co-operative ways of working and the beginning of a new vision for the lay faithful at work. The denominations have not much time to make up their minds. Severe economic pressures are enforcing radical changes: the kind of changes that could have happened in a more creative way years ago when mission was last on the agenda and the churches had more strength.

HOPE FOR INDUSTRIAL MISSION

I still envisage the continuation and development of Industrial Mission into the next century. Thirty years of good work in which signs of the Holy, Creative, Empowering, Reconciling and Truthful Spirit have been clearly evident, are not easily forgotten or swept away. Industrial Missions must not lose heart because church financial resources are shrinking and the 'old guard' is retiring. Change always gives opportunity for something new. Provided resources are available and the right kind of people are attracted to it, IM will continue to offer the church a sharp cutting-edge in the world and in its internal life. But things will alter.

I expect IM to change its 'industrial' image and to broaden its base to include what Roman Catholics call 'the world of work'. It is the Christian perception of the importance of work in God's creation which provides the key theological base for IM. It has never been right to deny those who work, but in other than factories, the support, insights and opportunities IM can give. The problem for IM, as for the nation, is to retain an industrial base within a wider field of operations.

I expect IM to become less clerical and more lay. As a doctrine of ministry develops which affirms the importance of the laity in their secular responsibilities in God's world, and their key role in ministry, it will become more obvious that economic systems cannot be changed to serve people except through those who are already in them. It has never been right, in a Christian sense, to define the laity in the negative, churchy terms of 'the non-ordained'. They have a role in ministry in their own right. Here IM, or whatever its new designation, will have three problems; to get the theologians on their side, to persuade the laity that they are equal partners with the ordained and to find a way of ministry that involves the powerful as well as the poor.

I expect IM to play a key role in developing a new sense of mission, a wider concept of worship and spirituality and a more effective way of nurturing Christians in their daily lives. As congregations are confronted by a Jesus for whom and through whom all things were created (Col 1:16), capture the biblical and prophetic call for universal justice and *shalom* (Isa 58, Mic 6:8, Amos 5:24), and see a vision to work for a Kingdom where all might have life (Luke 4:18, 19 and John 10:10), in the Third as well as the First World, the inadequacies of current unworldly evangelical and charismatic trends will be exposed. The church will need the insights and the spirituality that have fed IM all these years.

. . .

Rowland Goodwin is a Methodist minister, and was Senior Missioner of an ecumenical, eight-strong Industrial Mission team in Greater Manchester. He is now concentrating on the ministry of the laity and is Training Officer for Accompanied Self-Appraisal in the Manchester and Stockport District of the Methodist Church. He is author of *Living in the Fast Lane* (1991), a study programme to help church groups look at how Christians (especially those with management responsibilities) can address key 'faith and work' issues.

Ministry in secular employment (MSE)
Michael Ranken

Ministry of this kind is vital to the process of bringing the whole of life into the Kingdom of God.

There are now significant numbers of non-stipendiary ministers (NSMs) in most of the mainstream churches. Some earn their livings in other employment, some are retired, some are unemployed, some – homemakers, for instance – are in unpaid work. Amongst the NSMs there is a proportion who consider themselves MSEs, Ministers in Secular Employment ... The majority of NSMs, in all the denominations, are 'parish-focused' in their ministry. They

... see themselves, and are almost always seen by their churches, as more or less 'ordinary' ministers of religion who happen to have other jobs as well. The time and energy available to ministry in the congregation are limited by the demands of the other job, but otherwise what they are and do is not much different from any other parish minister. The ministry of MSEs, on the other hand, is 'work-focused'. Ministry in the congregation can be very important, fruitful and satisfying, to the congregation and to the MSE, but it is not the main ministry. That is in the day-to-day work.

...

An MSE who is employed by the institution to work at the institution's tasks may choose to function as an unofficial chaplain, doing some of the things, in similar ways and for similar purposes, as an official chaplain. But that is not what she is paid for. The institution, whose proper concern is for what the MSE is paid to do, may indeed welcome and support the extra-curricular ministry, yet many remain indifferent or even hostile. An MSE acting as a chaplain cannot have the independence of an outsider and so is largely disqualified from those parts of a chaplain's role where the work itself, and relationships among the people doing the work, are involved. His chaplaincy role is likely, therefore, to be largely restricted to private counselling, spiritual guidance and pastoral care, reinforced perhaps by conducting occasional religious services among his companions.

MINISTRY *IN* SECULAR EMPLOYMENT

But there is a different model of the MSE at work – of the minister operating not alongside the work but fully within it. Whereas the chaplain's task ... is to serve as a channel of spiritual strength from the church into the work to which he is a visitor, this kind of MSE takes full responsibility for his share in the work that has to be done. He seeks while doing it to recognize and to co-operate with the God who is already there, creating, redeeming and sustaining, in the work itself.

In churches we are accustomed to the notion that God, and the grace of God, are to be found everywhere and in everything – which must include the work we have to do. At work we need to discover that that is truly so, to proclaim it when we see it and then to enjoy it, with others, to celebrate the presence of God and the holiness of life in our work ... Of course, not everything at work is good and holy. We cause pain, suffering, injustice and hurt ... To see or to share in the suffering is to see or share in the experience of Christ. That is the story for the MSE to tell, once she sees it for herself ... The Good News of the Christian story is about passing through the wrong and the pain into New Life, redeemed, forgiven – always.

THE MSE IN CHURCH

In church ... we hear and tell the Christian story, mostly in the language and images of the Bible and church tradition, with occasional illustrations from 'ordinary' life thrown in. Jesus actually did it the other way round. His most powerful stories are not from Scripture or the synagogue tradition; they are about the ordinary people of his time doing the ordinary things they had to do, told by one who saw clearly the workings of the Kingdom of God within what they were doing ... The MSE, trained in church ways and practising them in church from time to time, must also be able to see and to celebrate and tell the same kind of stories in the language and images of that part of the 'ordinary' world to which he is committed, in the course of its ordinary working business.

Unfortunately, the church, by and large, does not seem to have yet grasped what is going on here ... MSEs still have to struggle hard themselves to discover what their ministry is and how to go about it. Yet I believe that ministry of this kind is vital to the process of bringing the whole of life into the Kingdom of God.

...

Michael Ranken is a food technologist and has spent a lifetime, until retirement in April 1997, in that industry. He was latterly a Partner in Micron Laboratories, a consultancy offering quality assurance services to manufacturers and traders in food. He was ordained in 1979, serves as Honorary Curate at St Martin's parish church, Epsom, and is a past Moderator of CHRISM (CHRistians In Secular Ministry).

The role of church leaders – a neglected ministry?
Michael Henshall

Church leaders who are willing to be out and about in the market place will rapidly discover that many of their deepest contacts are with those apparently farthest away from the church.

The bishop, the moderator, the chairman – by whatever title a church leader is known in his own back-yard – is in a unique and often privileged position to offer support to Christians (and others) in public life.

A SHIRT TO VALUE

In Church of England terms, some might argue that effectively all that is left of the Establishment is the purple shirt of the bishop. It opens doors. It opens significant conversations. It is oddly accepted in odd places. A wise wearer of such a significant shirt can become a prophet for the Kingdom. I often claim that my life is spent in pubs, palaces and prisons! In such contrasting establishments lurk unlimited gospel opportunities.

Sadly many church leaders become bedevilled with multitudinism. Busyness snuffs out any serious ministry to those beyond the ecclesiastical boundary. Preoccupation with 'the bloody machine' can of course provide a reason for not addressing the other. The management of the diary must leave good space for building contacts in the world of work.

We live in a society where residual public faith is not yet dead. The church leader who allows his or her diary to be dominated by total churchy-ness is letting slip innumerable opportunities. Whether it be from some incoherent apprehension of 'another country', from some fond remembrance of a Bible story told by a long departed mother in the nursery, or simply from some wobbly superstition, many do remain open to important informal discussions. In recent months, I call to mind significant conversations with a prison governor and the managing director of an international firm. Both encounters were built on a half-remembered faith and a residual memory.

A GAP IN OUR WITNESS

In my opening paragraph I deliberately place in parentheses the two little words 'and others'. I find that in the exercise of my public ministry many people come for conversations or seek supportive comments who are not committed to the Lord of the Gospel. Some even, like Nicodemus, come 'by night' not willing even to admit to others that they have 'talked to the church'. Others arrive with a sort of community agenda that conceals either personal spiritual need, or a *cri de coeur* from the midst of some ethical swamp.

Church leaders who are willing to be out and about in the market place will rapidly discover that many of their deepest contacts are with those apparently farthest away from the church and its ways. But not infrequently those farthest away paradoxically are nearer than they think to the Kingdom of God.

High on any list of major failings in the contemporary church is a massive dereliction of duty towards the world of work. We have failed to offer serious support to those in our congregations who spend many hours at work, often grappling with complicated moral dilemmas. We have been nearly as bad with those whom the economic system deprives of work. Boards of Social Responsibility may give birth to healthy reports on these subjects with which Synods delight to dabble, but the reality of support at the coal face is what counts.

Sunday after Sunday I listen in vain (usually) for the work-places and work problems of the congregation to figure in the intercessions. We go regularly on a Cook's Tour of the trouble spots of the globe, but of the trouble spots in the local factory or supermarket there is, alas, no mention.

Many of those carrying heavy responsibilities find to their dismay that so many church organizations which they attend simply serve up second-rate talks on topics like 'the flora and fauna of the Upper Zambezi'! Where there should be a forum for debate and mutual support on the issues of work, or no work, there is but a trivial pursuit.

A MAJOR SHIFT

A prime task for any church leader, before he or she engages in what must always be a limited personal ministry, is to teach, challenge, preach, convince the clergy that the local church must set out its stall to offer effective support to those in public life, whether dustmen on the local garbage van, or a major politician with 'gravy train' problems. Many clergy need to be involved in fresh theological thinking about the nature of the Kingdom in order to change direction. Others need help in resisting the allurement of busyness in order to have space for the essential task of seeing that those in the world of work are resourced in their Christian commitment and insight.

Lip service to the Decade of Evangelism engages in lofty talk about shifting the priorities of the local church from maintenance to mission. Attention to Christians exercising responsibility in the world of work must be one of these priorities. As secularism closes in, it is tempting to retreat into the false security of some gathered sect. But the fullness of God's world includes 'out there', includes the work place, the market place. We need to do more than keep the rumour of God alive by displays of tokenism. We need to enable the apostolate of the laity.

SUPPORTING GATEKEEPERS

In my job description there occurs the somewhat pompous expression 'To exercise a ministry to top people'. The theologian John Atherton, acting as my supervisor in a course for church leaders some years ago, strongly challenged the reality of that statement. He applauded it as an ideal. He questioned it as a sustainable policy. But how did it operate?

If they will only take it, church leaders still possess the clout to develop an effective ministry to the world of work and especially to its leaders. Two examples:

At present (1992), I host a series of lunches around the Diocese of Liverpool. They are made up of the leaders of industry, commerce, education and police. They take on board the chief executives of towns in the region and others with significant portfolios in the area. A leading firm like British Nuclear Fuels, or Laporte, or AEA Technology, or Vulcan Engineering pays for the lunch. Between 15 and 30 people meet regularly, for two and a half hours. The agenda usually bears on the moral and spiritual issues facing top management, or it takes the form of what might be termed 'supportive' talk. We have tried mixing such gatherings with Union representatives, but with little success.

In 1986, I put a lot of episcopal energy into Industry Year. I became Chairman of the Churches Section for the North West. Over 800 leaders of industry and commerce accepted my invitation to a major conference. My contacts with many of their firms has gone on with the years.

PRIORITIES

Church leaders today will tell of the incredible demands that come their way. In addition to 'the care of all the churches' (with jumpy congregations concerned with massive financial problems, and with a multitude of other problems) there are incessant demands from the media and from the community.

It is absolutely essential, therefore, for church leaders to have clear priorities supported by realistic objectives. Before all else we must keep open the windows 'towards Jerusalem', and set aside time for reading and reflection. The church leader must then make clear choices. Among my own key objectives are two that seem to matter more than many if the church's witness is to extend beyond the confines of the Christian congregation:

* to help clergy and parishes to support the world of work;
* to make definite opportunities to meet with Christians in public life in order to engage in open debate and to offer support.

Michael Henshall was formerly Bishop of Warrington in the Diocese of Liverpool. He has now retired but continues to take an active interest in church and society relationships.

PART III

Changing society

If a new understanding of Christian faith, of Christian mission, and of the life and organization of the church in today's world are brought to bear on the fundamental issues of our time, what difference might it make? The most compelling answer is that given by Christians actively engaged in the life of our society. This third set of papers draws on their first-hand experiences, concerns and insights first in a personal and then a societal context.

Personal perspectives

What does it mean to be a Christian seeking to express one's faith in everyday life? What are the questions raised and the responses attempted? What is the heart of the message we try to communicate, and what lessons are learnt along the way? How do we feel when we are so often out on our own? And where is the strength and support gained which enables us to be faithful to our calling?

Politics and faith

Hilary Armstrong

... the great principle that socialists and Christians have in common is a belief in a moral system.

Brought up in a Methodist and a Socialist household, religion and politics have always seemed a natural part of my life. I went to chapel and Sunday School and Labour Party meetings, and am still involved quite fully in the life of the Methodist Church. Methodism is an integral part of my public life, integral because my faith has informed and sustained the political creed which is the reason I wanted to become an MP in the first place. Methodism and Socialism, for me, are so thoroughly and so organically intertwined that in my life they are virtually inseparable in their influence.

For me the great principle that socialists and Christians have in common is a belief in a moral system. Democratic Socialism sprang from a firm moral underpinning which has a concern for the well-being of others as its first principle. The values of democratic Socialism, founded on a belief in the importance of society and solidarity, are closely intertwined with those of Christianity. It is not only a personal responsibility to behave justly and charitably towards other people but a political responsibility, that of ensuring that government accepts responsibility for the well-being of citizens and takes the opportunities open. In accepting our responsibilities towards citizens, particularly vulnerable groups, seriously, I believe we are recognizing a Christian responsibility.

A second link which informs my religious and political beliefs is the concept of community. The seventeenth-century poet and Dean of St Paul's, John Donne, warned his congregation in a famous sermon 'Do not send to see for whom the bell tolls, it tolls for thee'. Each man's death, he said, diminishes me, for no man is an island. We are all interlinked, part of the body of the church and part of the body politic, the social order. What more elegant refutation could there be of Margaret Thatcher's notorious pronouncement that there was 'no such thing as society'? What more elegant exposition of the social theory of community and interdependency?

The third link which connects my political and religious beliefs is the idea of equality of opportunity and development. Socialists believe profoundly that every child should have the opportunity of a good education, and that we are all entitled to be able to make the most of the gifts God has given us, whatever those gifts might be. We believe that we must work towards building a society which offers such opportunities to all its people, not just the wealthy or the fortunate. The impetus behind this is partly moral – based on ideas of justice and fairness – and partly pragmatic – that society cannot afford to waste the talents of its members by neglect or prejudice. Such beliefs are also profoundly Christian. I would go a step further and say that the belief that skills and talents are a grace which should properly be shared with others, by working as a member of the community, not only for personal satisfaction and gain, but also for the good of that community, is a common thread running through Christianity and Socialism. It is no coincidence that Third World charities are full of volunteers from the churches and from the political left. Indeed the crucible for my own political commitment was the two years I spent doing VSO work in Kenya.

Hilary Armstrong has been the Labour MP for North West Durham since 1987. She is a member of the Methodist Church, and Treasurer of the Methodist Division of Education and Youth.

Faith and politics – a personal reflection
Alistair Burt

I have always found it impossible to separate my faith from a sense of duty which has been made manifest in a commitment to public service.

... The home I was brought up in was one where duty and service abounded, though it was taken so much for granted that no one ever mentioned it. My father has recently retired after serving the community for 41 years as a family doctor. What he taught me in terms of service to all has stayed with me throughout my life. My mother worked in the home. She had two boys to bring up, as well as deal with the extra work which is part of a family doctor's life. Whatever else she might have wanted to do, it had to fit into a context in which other people's interests were placed first. This too has had a profound effect upon me. A sense of God was also present, notably from my father whose quiet Christian faith took us regularly to our local parish church. It was a home of talk and discussion, where I learned relatively early that my parents were Conservatives with a large *and* small 'c', a recipe for both tension and entertainment as I approached my slightly left-wing teenage years!

. . .

Deciding on a political orientation involves a variety of factors, not least background and development. God's world is full of choice and diversity – it is no surprise that it is so in politics!

. . .

It became essential to seek to understand what I was for. It seemed to me common sense, and not un-Christian, that a man or woman was properly rewarded in life for their skill and their effort. An economic system that understood this seemed likely to succeed. From a background of a father who worked in the health service, I was also acutely aware of the need for the system to provide for the less fortunate. We must, therefore, have a system of taxation which, whilst encouraging people and rewarding them for their efforts, ensures that the needs of those who cannot do so are provided for. The essential differences between a Conservative economic viewpoint and a fundamentally socialist economic viewpoint having been established, I found myself on the side of the Conservatives.

I still believe that traditional conservatism has a strong social content. The Conservative Party must continue to find opportunities, at the most grass-roots level, to ensure that people have the opportunity to do things for themselves rather than have things done for them. In public authority housing we already know of the impact that greater tenants' involvement can have in encouraging pride in their surroundings and determination in dealing with problems. Socialism had begun to sap the will of too many, and enormous strides have been made in tenants' involvement which I believe will pay many dividends. Similarly, the devolution of greater responsibility to individual schools, to the heads, teachers and governors, is also producing a revolution in attitude from those who too often had to accept the view of a county hall which was remote from them. There are always difficult balances to achieve between community and individual rights, but I certainly believe that the Conservative Government since 1979 has done much to correct a severe imbalance towards the state which had existed before.

. . .

The wheel of politics constantly turns – to right, then to left. So long as Christians are actively and passionately involved, so long as they keep a reference point for their politics above the merely secular, we should not worry. But we should pray for their influence in all parties to grow and flower.

Alistair Burt was Member of Parliament for Bury North from 1983 to 1997.

... also God's children?

Evelyn Jones

Are not the abusers also God's children?

I was overwhelmed by what I was learning. Quietly I listened, my heart swelling up within me, as little Katie, only seven years old, related to me her story which led to her being brought into care. It was her Mum's boyfriend. He had abused her and her sister many times.

'My sister liked it, but I didn't.' Was I hearing straight? I remembered my own daughter at seven – happy, bright, innocent. I would have felt like tearing apart anyone who had laid a finger on her in that way.

'Did Mummy know?' I asked tentatively. 'Oh yes. He did it to her, too.' Father God, how can I help this child? She called that man 'Daddy'.

James is eight. In his play he is obsessed with bonfires and killing and blood. He talks about demons and giants and having super strength and super power. Although obviously intellectually able, he still cannot read or write. His behaviour is often bizarre and very aggressive. We know he has been subject to gross neglect. Experts suspect ritualistic abuse, too.

I know, only too well, that Katie and James are not alone. Thousands of children throughout the country and across every stratum of society are suffering abuse at the hands of those who should be protecting them. Belonging to a church provides no immunity, either. Child abuse is a disease of our time and probably of many past generations, too, but at last it is being rooted out. There is the hope! We are starting to listen to children and believe what they are saying.

But, are not the abusers also God's children? Can we, while facing the distress of a child victim, also show compassion to those who cause it? And what about ritualistic abuse? We know that the victory of good over evil has been won, but evil practices involving children still go on and the results are often tragic. To ignore that is to do so at our peril.

The only Christian response must be to love with all our hearts, to bear the pain with both the abused and the abuser and to offer, as far as our flawed natures will allow, the same unconditional love that Christ gives to us.

Evelyn Jones was Officer-in-Charge of a specialist residential unit in Worcestershire, caring for abused children. She is now a play therapist working with severely disturbed and damaged children.

True and fair

Alison Lusty

Behind all accounts are people.

Reflecting a business via the apparently factual medium of a set of accounts is an art rather than a science. By careful book-keeping we can tell how the business uses its cash, how much it has invoiced its customers, how much its creditors are asking for payment. But how do we know which customers will not pay, or for how much a huge claim from a creditor will be settled? Accounts are full of judgements which can so easily be twisted by half truths and clever arguments. The Chartered Accountancy profession seeks to impose its high standards of integrity and professionalism in this moral maze.

Published accounts are a balancing act between the company's natural optimism and the auditor's inherent pessimism. Somewhere between the two lies the balance at which the auditors are able to express, in the required audit report, that the accounts show a 'true and fair view'. In my view it is much easier to make judgements and balance the viewpoints from a Christian perspective than being purely ruled by a professional ethic founded on pessimism. Such a temptation to skew the truth is contrary to Christian integrity. Behind all accounts are people. And a decision to cut overheads unnecessarily can be jobs lost. A decision to improve productivity means that someone will be at the unemployment benefit office tomorrow, as too many people are aware in this current recession.

In November 1991 the group of companies I was working for went into receivership. Suddenly old lines of authority were cut. The receivers occupied the MD's suite, intercepted the incoming post, scrutinized the outgoing post and wandered round in droves collecting information to sell the underlying businesses. The receivers were for the most part young and thrusting, ruling with their ultimate weapon of dismissal without the rules of compensation that apply in a solvent company. People who had worked all their lives in the group suddenly lost their livelihood and their reason for self-esteem. At the end of each working week selected employees were collected in offices, handed their redundancy notices. Some were seen wandering along the familiar corridors for the last time with tears running down their faces.

I worked for three months for the receivers and have now moved to a new career. But what about the people who have all their working life apparently wasted in a failed firm? It is only from the perspective of a Christian life that any hope can be found. Only, I believe, in this context does it become clear that no experience is wasted, that even in the deepest darkness there is always a glimmer of hope. God's truth prevails even if life is not always fair.

Alison Lusty is a Chartered Accountant who is currently Group Chief Accountant of a large PLC based in Birmingham.

Towards quality of service
David Pinwell

... working effectively together in an open, honest atmosphere of mutual trust ... has clear parallels with the Gospel.

Companies are increasingly turning to 'Total Quality Management' as a means of improving their competitiveness in the market-place. This is based on the recognition that customers will go where they are well treated and receive quality goods or services.

Such programmes also recognize the importance of staff on the 'front line' of a business. Principles of treating employees as people, showing respect and caring for them, and recognizing that everyone at all levels of an organization has much more potential to contribute, are emerging as keys to success.

As a result, companies are investing in training to improve the 'communications' and 'people' skills of their staff and in 'team building'. They are also recognizing that those who understand the real day-to-day problems that affect quality of service are those who work 'on the shop floor', and are appointing them to 'quality teams' with the responsibility for achieving real improvements. This is nothing new. For many years Marks and Spencer and similar companies have built their success on this approach. And it emerges from the work of management scientists like Abraham Maslow, Frederick Herzberg and Douglas McGregor almost half a century ago.

But, perhaps more to the point, these trends towards working effectively together in an open, honest atmosphere of mutual trust and helping each other to 'realize their potential', as advocated today by TQM consultants, has clear parallels with the Gospel that we preach. These qualities of mutual respect, brotherhood and love for each other, standing not in judgement but in support, as limbs of the same body, that we aspire to through our Christian faith, have been found to be a foundation for successful working together in employment.

But some die-hard old school managers find it all too difficult to swallow. They believe that the 'strength' of a manager comes in remaining aloof, keeping employees in the dark and motivating by fear. This being so much easier than having to demonstrate the 'weakness' of 'being human after all'.

It is surely here that Christians, following in the footsteps of Jesus who showed the nature of true strength in the ultimate way, can exercise real leadership by example. So I, for one, embrace the TQM approach wholeheartedly, giving it full support within my own company, and continue to encourage love and brotherhood in relationships as a foundation for effective teamwork and individual growth. But at the same time I ask whether we, as a church, have something to learn from TQM initiatives. We are called through the Gospel to respond to God's call, to serve and to witness. Most of us find ourselves hopelessly unequal to the task. We endeavour to work together effectively in fellowship, but frequently feel that we fail.

So, as we take our understanding and belief from our Christian fellowship into the workplace, is there room for us to bring the learning of the workplace back into the church? Perhaps we, too, should be making some investment in communications, 'people' skills and team building. For without these we might not be able to fulfil our full potential for discipleship.

David Pinwell manages the information services team of an international Communications Products company from its Birmingham headquarters.

Councillor who ...?
Andrew Coulson

The role of a Christian is ... to make judgements with integrity and to support those who cannot and will not speak for themselves.

Councillors are given every chance to exaggerate their self-importance. But in Birmingham there are 117 of us, part-time volunteers, and 53,000 paid employees, some earning more than most councillors can dream of. We cannot be on top of all the detail that concerns these employees. And in truth most of what happens in council committees involves no more than asking a few polite questions and then voting through whatever has been carefully prepared and packaged by the council's paid officers.

So why do it? Why spend all that time just to be the butt of every comedian's jokes? What, if anything, has it got to do with Christian commitment?

There are certainly large sums of money involved – never enough – so deciding what should be cut and what resourced is important. It means employment rather than unemployment for some – a free service, not a free service, or no service at all for others.

Anyone elected a councillor becomes the person who carries the can, speaking up as best she or he can to the media or the public meeting when things go wrong, taking the credit when things go well, and trying to feed back constructive suggestions or ideas to officers who might develop them or put them into practice. So it does need people with certain talents – stubbornness, thick skins, perception, patience, loyalty, a common touch, a sense of honour, ability to quickly identify the key features of a complex situation. It also requires time – lots of it.

The role of a Christian in all this is perhaps no more than to make judgements with integrity, and to support those who cannot or will not speak for themselves. And above all to place decisions in context. The temptation for councillors (made worse by the feelings we have of powerlessness and isolation) is that we come to think that we are special. That we have given up time, and in return are entitled to be a bit pompous and to make the most of fringe benefits such as banquets, free tickets and foreign trips. The more this happens, the more it undermines the basis of local democracy – that elected members should represent, and be one with, their constituents.

Andrew Coulson, an economist by training, has lectured at Birmingham University since 1984 and been a Labour Councillor for Selly Oak in Birmingham since 1990.

Train – or no tomorrow
Kathleen Carey

Training is something to which I am particularly committed.

Work in the construction industry of which my company is part has been severely hit in recent years. The lack of development in our cash-starved communities has meant too many people chasing too few contracts; creating lowered pricing, lack of sufficient profitability and, in extreme cases, receivership with its disastrous effects on so many lives. Recession brings out the worst in characters as each company fights for survival. In a number of instances it is unfair competition which gains the contract.

Being a director in a small company relates to having an extended family of 35. Each is unique, sharing joys and sorrows. My company has, for the past seven years, released me from usual company duties one day each week, to work on a voluntary basis helping build the confidence of people whose lives have been shattered by mental illness, depression and sadness. It is to this group of people I owe a great debt. They have taught me how to listen with compassion and accept my frailty along with theirs. The wide diversity of the two jobs has helped me accept and respond to life with all its joys as well as knocks.

Training is something to which I am particularly committed. I am partly responsible for all structured training within the company. Whilst realizing we are in a world recession, I believe the Government needs to look even more closely at the long-term effect which will be caused by the lack of present day skilled training. At a recent business seminar, one man publicly declared that he would not train others again as it was too expensive, but would 'poach' skilled labour trained by others. I thought at the time that his opinion was unusual but, having heard the latest training figures in the electrical industry, his attitude evidently is not uncommon.

The Government must also look to investing money in our schools and other public buildings in order to create jobs in the deflated construction industry and once more boost training. We have the structures in place via the Training and Enterprise Councils, but these can only work effectively if sufficient cash is allocated and more companies motivated.

I trust that, through the grace of God, my relationship with the Training and Education Committee of the MCCI (Manchester Chamber of Commerce and Industry) and with the Greater Manchester Industrial Mission Council will enable me to play some small part in keeping training and the future of young people to the forefront. One of my dearest wishes, however, is to witness the church truly linking all employed/unemployed life to Sunday worship. Industrial Mission seems to be left to a handful of people when such an important part of life should be the concern of us all.

Kathleen Carey is a Company Director with Carey Electrical Engineering. She is a member of the Church of England.

Issues of integrity
Malcolm Claydon

... God's call to me to be 'salt and light' in the place and in the situation into which he has put me.

Some time ago, at an Institute dinner, as I sat with a group of colleagues, customers and one or two suppliers, the person next to me turned and said 'What's a nice guy like you doing in a place like this?'

This was not a very original comment but since he knew of my Christian faith, I was aware of what he was getting at. By 'nice' I guess he meant 'innocent' or 'naïve', and by 'a place like this' I suppose he was referring to the succession of blue jokes to which the after-dinner speakers were subjecting us. I have often asked myself the same kind of question. If I were called to be a member of the clergy, or some other instantly recognizable member of the 'God Squad' then I could easily have withdrawn from such gatherings and no one would have been surprised. No such luck!

The fact is, I have always regarded the whole of my life, including my paid employment, as 'full-time service' for God. It follows, therefore, that if God calls me to work in a particular industry, I believe I should not only do that work to the best of my ability, but get fully involved in the business and particularly with the people in it. If that means occasionally subjecting my ears to a bombardment of things I might otherwise avoid, then so be it.

Much more important is God's call to me to be 'salt and light' in the place and in the situation into which he has put me. This involves a constant struggle to maintain standards of honesty and integrity in an environment where lies, deceit and politics are commonplace. What do you do for example, when a customer pays an invoice twice in error and your company decides to say nothing; or when a supplier demands payment on an overdue account and your cash-flow means that he will not be paid for some time yet? Tell him the cheque is in the post? Issues like these are commonplace for many of us and they are often not that clear cut. A steadfast refusal to get involved with office politics has been a further issue that I have had to address. I know of several Christians whose careers have suffered because they have abstained from such activities.

In all these things, I wish I could say that I have never failed. I can't! However, I have found a daily sense of the Lord's presence with me in all situations and his guidance just when I needed it most. This in turn has given me the most important thing of all: an insight into what are the real priorities and a clear distinction between the things that are eternally important and those which simply occupy us from day to day.

Malcolm Claydon is a Company Director working in the automotive components industry. He is an Anglican.

Faith in the inner city
Janette Stebbens

Only rarely do urban congregations recognize ... this wealth of theological insight which comes ... from those ... who choose to stay outside our religious institutions ...

Birmingham City Council launched its city-wide Anti-Poverty Initiative in 1992. This followed a 'pilot' initiative which focused on Ladywood, an inner-city estate situated just behind Birmingham's prestigious International Convention Centre. This location provided stark contrasts between those who could afford to spend comparatively large sums of money on entertainment and hotel bills and those who, because of poverty, were struggling to keep pace with life on the margins. One of the main aims of the local initiative was: 'To identify and assess those barriers, at the local level, which prevent people who are disadvantaged from participating fully in economic and social activity.'

It was both exhilarating and heart-warming to be part of a local debate which, whilst seeking to recognize the wide-ranging effects of economic hardship, also acknowledged society's growing 'culture of contentment' which, dependent as it is on people's purchasing power, seemed also to relegate vast numbers of people to anonymity and non-participation in public life.

My daytime work involves me in the setting up of support networks for local families who spend much of their creative energy struggling to survive on state benefit. This experience often leads to alienation or despair, but I am constantly encouraged by a significant minority of local residents who, despite their own financial worries, still manage to make important contributions to the well-being of their local community. I have occasionally enquired about the source of their motivation and a number, perhaps surprisingly, have confided in me the importance of their own faith – a faith which seems to have been passed on to them by oral family tradition rather than through formal church teaching.

My own observations have led me to believe that their experiences of poverty and powerlessness have provided them with insights into the gospel stories which are denied to those of us who are buttressed by employment, home ownership and insurance policies. Jesus, I believe, stood where they are now standing and told his stories from their perspective. I could relate many real-life incidents which would serve as modern-day parables, but only rarely do urban congregations recognize and affirm this wealth of theological insight which comes, not from those who are to be found standing confidently 'at the front' of our churches, but from those who sit quietly and passively in the pews or who choose to stay outside our religious institutions altogether. Theirs is an experience which cannot be gained from books!

A question remains. Are the barriers which prevent the disadvantaged from participating fully in social and economic activity the same as those which prevent the full and active theological participation of 'ordinary' people in the life of the local church? If so, doesn't the Gospel have something to say on the matter?

Janette Stebbens was Joint Project Co-ordinator of the Ladywood Project (funded by Birmingham City Council). She is now Senior Youth and Community Worker at Ladywood Community and Health Centre, Birmingham. She describes herself as 'vaguely Anglican'.

'Light in a dark place'?
Paul Cooper

... making a small change in others' perceptions of Christians.

'You know, you're an odd sort of bloke to be a Christian'.

'What do you mean?"

'Well surely religious people are usually elderly women or people with problems!'

This comment was made to me by my boss of sixteen years ago in the multinational electronics company where I still work.

My early contacts with the church were baptism (of which I remember nothing!) and when I was confirmed at age twelve. Confirmation went along with various inoculations and the eleven-plus exam and was just one of a number of events which, although variously painful, had no immediate effect. By the time I was studying physics at university, I could be described as a militant agnostic whose view of Christians had much in common with those of my future boss. My conversion to Christ came after graduation while studying for a doctorate.

I joined my present company 21 years ago. Now I had to come to terms with spending the major part of each day in an environment where, as far as I knew, I was the only Christian. Furthermore the company had and still has a substantial part of its business in the 'defence' market. This has given me pause for thought over the years. Many of the electronic systems we produce become the control and communication elements of military systems as well as being used in the medical, oil or space industries. We live in a world where people have largely cut themselves off from God and in which the potential for evil is ever present. Developments in electronics have enabled more accurate and selective weapon systems. War is a wretched and messy option, yet in a fallen world such action is sometimes necessary. This has been so from the battles described in Old Testament times to the conflicts yet to come before the prophecy in Revelation 21 is fulfilled.

Some people have seen my position in industry as a great opportunity to be 'light in a dark place'. In practice it is not quite like that! There is a challenge to maintain Christian integrity but this is coupled with doubts and frustrations leading to the thought that people in some softer working environments will find it easier. For me, the main joy has been in making a small change in others' perceptions of Christians. I have found that as I gain people's confidence, they have sometimes opened up to me when they find life difficult. We never know the effect of our words and attitudes. A former colleague was the Christian speaker at a dinner I attended, and yet when we shared the same workplace I would never have had the faith to believe that he would come to Christ. My hope is that people with whom I work will continue to think that I'm an 'odd sort of bloke to be a Christian'.

Paul Cooper is the Research Manager of an electronics company and a member of an evangelical Anglican church.

The school – a community of work and worth

Sue Gibbons

We all have gifts, are of worth, and build up our shared community.

In one sense it makes not the slightest difference that I am a *Christian* earning my living as a teacher. I am not employed in a church school, and I am not an RE specialist, so I do not have any kind of explicit Christian label which is directly connected with my job description. However, in another sense, faith and work have inextricably merged together in all that I do in the school where I teach 13–18-year-olds.

As a Christian belonging to a church community in the area where I live, I take the body of Christ as my model for that community. I believe that we can only function fully as individuals when we recognize that we are parts of the whole body, with our various gifts being shared for the benefit of all. I hang on to that when I am at work, because if the idea matters at all, it matters *wherever* people are.

For example, I cannot function very well in my classroom if it is dirty. So our cleaners are crucial to the well-being of both the students and myself. A couple of years ago, when privatization of cleaning services in schools created a great deal of uncertainty and insecurity, it was a case of reaffirming the worth of all parts of the school body. Non-teaching staff needed to know that they mattered as people and that their work for others was valued, both financially and in its benefit to others. David Jenkins once wrote (1988, pp. 76–7): 'What does the church exist for? My short answer to that is: "To celebrate and promote worth in the name of God the Holy Trinity" ... Worth is what God sees in us.' If paid employment is to do with how we use our time and talents, how part of our 'worth' is realized, then that influences my relationships with all for whom and with whom I work.

During the past twelve months, I have often felt that my worth as a teacher has been undermined by changes stemming from central government. Ironically, I have welcomed initiatives such as the National Curriculum and Teacher Appraisal – often it is not change in itself which is bad but the way in which it is managed. Changes which are imposed too quickly, in large quantities, with limited consultation and few opportunities for training or adjustment, tend to fragment individuals and communities, denying them a full sense of worth.

Schools have increasingly had to see themselves in competitive economic terms, marketing themselves and their products in the most 'attractive' way possible. Careful management of resources is what the church often describes as good stewardship, and is as much a practical part of caring for the body in both church and schools terms. But perhaps we go too far when we see the cheapest financial cost as unquestionably the best value, and the highest examination attainment grades as the only criteria for 'success' in published league tables. I celebrate the top grades for those students who are capable of gaining them, but there are those who have actually achieved more when they get the lowest grade!

All our students are part of the school, along with teachers, ancillary staff, cleaners, caterers, caretakers, governors, parents ... We all have gifts, are of worth, and build up our shared community. That, for me, is of God.

Sue Gibbons is a senior teacher at a comprehensive school in Redditch, Worcestershire, and an Anglican priest in the Diocese of Worcester.

At the 'crossroads'
Ruth Stables

Committing the whole day to God ...

7 a.m. – and the news on the radio tries to penetrate my still deep sleep. After the struggle to get up, I spend ten minutes in prayer, committing the whole day to God – an increasingly valuable time this – too short – shouldn't I get up earlier and spend longer?

8.45 a.m. – arrive at work after a ten-minute drive. I greet my colleagues – an important part of establishing relationships each day – and am then greeted by my office – paper everywhere – not the image of order and peace I strive to create – bless this mess! Have I got my priorities right, though? Looking at me from my noticeboard is a cut-out clown's face – reminding me that perhaps sometimes at work I need to be 'a fool for God' – putting him first above everything. That means doing my job as well as I can – seeing my work as Service Quality Manager as an integral part of my vocation.

'What are you doing this weekend?' linked with 'How is your other job?' is a question I am often asked. I always answer that I see it all as one job. I am a priest wherever I am – it is integral to everything I do. A monk once said he realized after many years that it was no good putting off prayer until the paperwork had been cleared off the desk – the prayer was *in* the paperwork.

Less of the paperwork. That isn't what fires me up – it's people – feeling I'm in the business of buying quality health-care services for people. That involves listening to them, looking at the service provided from their point of view – putting people first, constantly asking challenging questions – and always at the back of my mind asking what would Christ's attitude have been? Clearly I have to work *through* the organizational structure. But that needs to be dynamic so that it can adapt and yet always put the patient at the centre.

9 a.m. – sees me at a contract monitoring meeting with one of the large directorates in the local hospital trust. It's good to be here – talking to a consultant clinical director, senior nurse manager and business manager. Before becoming a purchaser I had been a provider for years and I think I understood many of the problems and tensions for providers – but also the opportunities. Perhaps I am seen, therefore, as quite a challenge. I know too much, ask too many questions. Yet I have to remember I am a purchaser now – it's their job to run the Trust, ours to say what we want to buy with the money available. When we have discussed progress on activity, we turn to quality issues, often centred on the Patient's Charter. We talk about how the service is being delivered – not just what. I think that is just as important – and I am anxious to be fair – to give credit where it is due. But to say when I do not think the standards reached are acceptable. We also ask about future developments – how can health care be improved?

I can see the stresses and strain on people's faces as I encourage and cajole them to make better use of resources, to be more efficient and effective in meeting the Patient's Charter standards, e.g. no one to wait more than 30 minutes in an out-patient clinic. 'Do you want me to limit how long I give to my patients?' says the consultant. Do I? We both know the patient has maybe waited weeks for that 'life-event' appointment. I really want to say that that patient should have as long as is clinically – and personally – necessary. Yet we both know there are many more patients to see and that the ideal may not be achieved. And I am the person associated with incentives and penalties in relation to the standard.

There is always the struggle to provide 'the excellent service' and I often come away from these meetings frustrated. As purchaser, my colleagues and I are always pressurized for more money, for more staff, more equipment. How can we meet these quality standards without more? Yet how well are current resources being used? We can all see that services can be improved – and we rarely use the world 'rationing'. But isn't that what we have always done one way or another? Difficult choices *have* to be made – and it's uncomfortable – but hasn't the truth to be faced and told openly and honestly and the public treated as adults and involved in these choices? Isn't that about God's justice and love?

11 a.m. – and I'm off on a Quality visit to our local Psychiatric Unit. Whenever I go on a visit, I have one main question: 'Would I want this service for my relatives/friends/self?' I try and stand outside my official role, which in many ways can see all the reasons why things can't be improved, and say 'Why can't they be improved?' 'What is preventing the provision of a perfect service?' It is often attitudes rather than resources but staff, understandably, can easily think I am being critical of them when they are doing their best within the framework they have been given. In many ways they need affirming in what they do. I have to assure them that, as purchasers, we need to know and see where the shortfalls are because that brings alive what we purchase – and could change our priorities. I am not sure I always convince them! But I need to work to build up that confidence and trust between purchaser and provider. It's a partnership really.

Often, again, I feel quite angry and frustrated inside at the end of a Quality visit – there is so much more that could be done. Need stares me in the face. More often, I am humbled and I come away full of admiration for staff working in an environment I could not handle. Where is God in all this? I've seen his love many times in the relationships between staff and patients, on the faces of staff, relatives and patients – that's a real privilege.

1 p.m. – back to the office to sort some papers out or read some report over lunch. Is all the paperwork relevant to what I have seen this morning? It is if it has a purpose. Resources have to be allocated. Services and organizations do not run on thin air – but the paperwork has to serve a purpose.

1.45 p.m. – and I am going to a meeting with local residents to listen to their views on the Health Authority's purchasing plan. It's quite a long document – and next time it needs to be written in a way that people can understand more easily. It's good to hear people's views directly. There is often no beating about the bush and what they want is refreshingly simple – if difficult to provide! Better car parking and signposts, shorter waiting times and waiting lists, more information. We are *public* servants, in the fullest sense of those words. Why aren't we more focused on the simpler things?

How can we respond? It's important, I believe, to go back to people and say what we have been able to change and what we would like to do but cannot do – yet – and give reasons. That's the hard bit – saying 'No' – but people respect honest sincere answers and we can't hide behind a bureaucratic face. It's important that we listen to how people really experience the service, that we are not protected. Christ wasn't protected. He saw people in their real need.

3.30 p.m. – and back to the office for a meeting with managers from the local Trust that provides community services. How can we, as purchasers, really monitor the service we are buying? What sort of right does Mrs Smith have to a chiropodist? How long does she wait? How long does Mr Smith have to wait for aids and adaptations to his home when he comes out of hospital? How can his wife, his unpaid carer, be helped to support him? What does community care *really* mean?

Of necessity, I have to look at the quality of service provided on a macro-level – the broad, horizontal view. It's also important, however, to drill down and examine individual scenarios – the vertical look – and that's when the un-comfortable questions emerge. It can be easy and comforting to be compla-cent, to cope by being 'over-positive', to look just at the many improvements and paper over the cracks. That's why the drilling down is important. And the model for that? The horizontal pierced by the vertical? For me, it's the Cross – the centre of the tensions, of the struggle – but through the Cross comes the Resurrection – new life, new hope – giving up is not an option.

7 p.m. – and I get home, tired, after trying to spend time in the office finish-ing today and preparing for tomorrow. I now try not to bring work home – a new departure for me – but there's too little time for family, friends and other interests. To be a balanced person I must not spend all my time at work. My effectiveness should not depend on the amount of time I spend at work. It's the *quality* of work I do when I am there that matters.

So, evening activities – meetings, seeing friends, swimming, catching up on personal correspondence – and then that precious time after 11 p.m. A time of quiet – for reading the daily paper, the Bible, thinking over the day and com-mitting all that has happened to God. It's good to journey inwards so that I have the energy to journey outwards the next day.

It's usually midnight or after when I drop exhausted into bed – always later than intended – is it any wonder the alarm clock penetrates my deep sleep? Have I really got the balance right? I guess I am still struggling – but I know that God is there in the midst of that struggle and that, whatever, I am held by His love.

Ruth Stables was Service Quality Manager with the North Staffordshire Health Authority. She now works part-time for the Diocese of Lichfield as Social Responsibility Officer and part-time with the North Staffordshire Health Authority as Assistant Commissions Manager: Priority Services. She serves as Assistant Curate in the parish of Knutton, Newcastle-under-Lyme.

Societal perspectives

Christians in public life are called to live out their faith not only on the personal level but also in an institutional context. They are dealing with 'principalities and powers' which, for better or for worse, affect the lives of many people in a profound way. Below are set out a selection of responses to current concerns made by Christians working in various sectors of our society.

Taxation not donation

Paul Nicolson

... economic justice for the poor is not voluntary in the Bible.

I was Director of the Church Urban Fund Appeal in the Diocese of Oxford. We lived in the days of the 'trickle down' theory of economic management. Give the rich massive tax cuts and the wealth creators their heads and the money needed by the poor will trickle down to them due to the increased capacity to give voluntarily granted to the wealthy. I am now ashamed that I fell for it. We, the Christians involved, should have asserted time and time again that economic justice for the poor is not voluntary in the Bible.

JUSTICE IS NOT VOLUNTARY

At the heart of modern corporate thinking is a view that economic justice for the poor is a matter of charity, which is thought to mean voluntary giving. There is, however, no such thing as voluntary giving to the hungry, homeless, sick and destitute in the Bible where economic justice is mandatory ... The claim that the biblical meaning of charity is an optional virtue is not true. In the Christian faith we are commanded to love. Love and charity are the same word. Sharing with the poor is a legal requirement in the Old Testament, like modern taxation. St Ambrose picks up the point.

> The earth is all men's, not the property of the rich, but those who use their own are fewer than those who lost the use of it. Therefore in alms you pay a debt, you do not bestow a bounty.

The business values of modern companies do not spell out this responsibility. Taxation rather than donations is the modern means by which economic justice is or is not established.

CHARITABLE DONATIONS AND LOTTERIES ARE NOT ENOUGH

Charitable donations and private enterprise have done nothing to slow down the increase in poverty over the past fifteen years in the United Kingdom. The proportion of gross income spent on charity declined from 0.85 per cent in 1987/88 to 0.6 per cent in 1990/91. State generosity in tax policy to the wealthy, amounting in many cases to over £20,000 a year, has not promoted sufficient corporate or private generosity to the poor and the homeless. On the other hand, the wealthy have set up family trusts for their children or set up accounts in overseas tax havens out of Nigel Lawson's tax decreases, while the government has taken the 16- and 17-year-old children of the poor out of benefit.

The Charities Aid Foundation reported in 1992 last year, 'The Government is making the assumption that people are giving more and that charities are able to play a greater role in caring for the needy. These figures are a clear warning that this is not happening.' Spectacular televised fund-raising events and the national lottery mask the need for a massive increase in government aid to the poor in this country and abroad.

No charity or lottery is big enough to cope with the needs of the hungry and destitute of the world. They rely, therefore, on Christians and others in multinational companies to draft, in their wisdom, their business values in a manner which will incorporate the biblical concept of economic justice to take account of their needs through national taxation. Christians are called to work for the common good. Taxation is the means through which the common good should be justly financed.

TAXATION AND BUSINESS VALUES

When companies write their business values they rightly emphasize the responsibility of the company towards the community. That responsibility could be extended to a consideration of the relationship between the taxes paid by the company and the financial needs of the poor. The National Consumer Council reported in 1992 that it is primarily lack of money that causes people to go without food or eat an inadequate diet in Britain. Despite official assertions to the contrary, all the detailed evidence shows that for many people a healthy diet is beyond their means. There is no published research by the Department of Social Security which disproves the available evidence of malnutrition. Add to this evidence of starvation in Britain the fact that a recent study reported by the Commission on Social Justice shows that the poor are dying younger and that the reasons given are stress, inadequate health care and inadequate diet, then it becomes clear that social benefits in the United Kingdom are inadequate ... The issue is whether or not multinational companies and tax paying individuals are willing to accept the challenge to incorporate a policy which promotes economic justice in their business values.

JUSTICE – THE COMMERCIAL AND BIBLICAL IMPERATIVE

In the United Kingdom the registered unemployed number regularly over 2.5 million, plus an estimated 1.5 million who are unemployed but not registered because they are not entitled to unemployment benefit, though they may be receiving another benefit. It is likely that unemployment will increase, even if the economy grows, due to the advent of the computer. Vacancies average about 400,000. The Department of Social Security states that it keeps benefit levels low lest they act as a disincentive to work. Benefits are now, however, far too low. There is a grave social danger in a permanent and growing pool of over 4 million people chasing 400,000 jobs while attempting to live below the bread line. Without biblical justice as part of their leader's wisdom nations stumble into instability and violence. It is the worst possible conditions of trade for all industries except the arms trade. The stock exchange prefers a stable world to an unsettled one.

Helder Câmara, a Bishop in South America, has described what he calls the spiral of violence. Hunger is the violence of the well-fed against the hungry. Next the hungry rebel violently at the injustice of their hunger. Then the forces of law and order, financed by the well-fed, violently repress the hungry. The way to break into this spiral is to implement justice by ensuring the hungry are fed in the first place. This vision of economic justice when put into practice will provide a peaceful society in which people may trade and create wealth and in which everyone may fulfil their God-given potential as human beings.

Paul Nicolson is a parish priest within the Hambledon Valley Group of Churches, Henley-on-Thames. He has long experience of the Church of England's ministry in secular employment, working in industry and with the Trades Unions. He has been a district councillor. He now works with voluntary organizations combating poverty and lobbying Parliament on behalf of the poor.

Christian perspectives on the social audit of commercial companies

Richard Adams

.. the Christian approach to social audit will look for a process which ... is consciously directed at encouraging positive social and spiritual values.

A small number of companies which accept that their social record is as or more important than the issue of financial return for shareholders have undertaken a social audit in the UK. A description of the process, by Ed Mayo, Director of the New Economics Foundation, may provide a helpful introduction for those unfamiliar with what is involved. He writes:

> In 1992, Traidcraft decided to commit itself to preparing an annual social audit and started work with the New Economics Foundation (NEF) to develop the way to do this ... The resulting social audit method was born out of a healthy mix of community-based participative research techniques and the literature of organizational development. At its core was a 'stakeholder' approach.
>
> Stakeholders are defined as those individuals and groups who are affected by, or can affect, the activities of the organization. On this basis, a social audit offers a means of assessing the social impact and ethical behaviour of an organization in relation to its stakeholders.
>
> The key facets of the social audit are:
>
> 1. Comparative – it offers a means whereby the performance of the organization can be compared to that of other related organizations.
> 2. Comprehensive – it sets out to provide a more comprehensive assessment of an organization's social impact and ethical behaviour.
> 3. Polyvocal – it is based on the views and accounts of stakeholders themselves, as well as those of the enterprise members. Thus, the approach is a 'social' document, reflecting the views of many groups.
> 4. Regular – it is intended to take place on a regular basis.
> 5. Externally validated – the results are validated by one or more people who do not have a vested interest in the results.
> 6. Disclosure – the results are disclosed to stakeholders.

The reasons why companies would undergo a social audit seem to go far beyond doing the right thing. It addresses the effectiveness of company activity by articulating different stakeholder values and perspectives, offers an invaluable guide for strategy planning and offers a means of accountability. However, rather than wait for the major companies to take the plunge, we believe that it is in the 'social economy' that the method will gain ground. We are taught to see community development work and ethical/green businesses as marginal to the main economy. In fact, this 'social economy' is both the basis and the demonstration of a more sane, socially just and environmentally sustainable economy.

NEF's social audit of Traidcraft, now in its third year, has been praised as being exceptionally thoroughgoing and genuinely open. But it has to be said that Traidcraft is a company which, more than most, has given considerable thought to its *raison d'être* and knows that it can count on the support of a sympathetic group of shareholders and customers. Not all companies can rely on this. Shareholders have a nasty habit of expecting short-term gains and if ethics – as opposed to what is statutorily required or what will not engender adverse publicity – get in the way of profit, then principles are usually regarded as a dispensable luxury.

CHRISTIAN PRINCIPLES

The Christian approach to business has been ambivalent and often culturally determined. When Adam Smith was defining the workings of the market in the second half of the eighteenth century, he referred to the process as being underpinned by a 'moral sentiment', a common set of values to which all decent people subscribed. For Smith this meant the Judaeo-Christian tradition, with a contemporary dash of the Enlightenment thrown in. Today, increasing cultural and moral relativism has meant we can no longer assume this is the case. But there is evidence that *discussion* about ethics, socially, politically and in business, is now on the increase. Christians need to be in the forefront of this debate and seek to influence it in a way which demonstrates an underlying concern about people as individuals and the creation as a gift in trust.

A distinctively Christian approach to social audit would therefore be looking for an underlying philosophy in a business that says that humanity must escape from an excessive emphasis on individualism and competition. We have to recognize the need for justice and ecological limits within our activities and these have to be internalized deep within the social fabric. This will mean exploring in a corporately self-critical way past failures. The ethic for all business must acknowledge that the resources and products of our planet belong to everyone; that individuals have an inalienable dignity, a right to self-realization and fulfilment; and that this will be expressed in a common good. Do the structures and processes of a company enable people to apply themselves constructively to the individual and common good, do they enhance the opportunity for them to act ethically, creatively and in a sustainable manner over the long term?

REFRAMING

This approach has to be apparent not just through a set of written statements but in the totality of the business itself. Of course we have to recognize areas of compromise, ideals deferred, contradiction and inconsistency. In recognizing these we recognize our own experience of life and hopefully prevent a moralizing element. Not only should a manufacturing company indicate that it has developed a responsible approach to its use of resources but retailers will need to address some of the fundamental problems of consumerism. We need to re-define consumer confidence as the confidence to choose to possess less and to choose to possess, where possible, for the common good. We have to challenge the idea that self-realization and personal fulfilment are linked with acquiring, that 'being' is not the same as 'having'. Of course, when put like this the idea sounds naïve, idealistic and more than a little sanctimonious but it is possible to see how this might be worked out in practice. We are inevitably involved in buying, having and consuming, but the Christian approach to social audit will look for a process which, instead of supporting a system which takes more than it gives and which ignores adverse impacts on society and the environment, is consciously directed at encouraging positive social and spiritual values.

Richard Adams was formerly Director of the business research charity New Consumer. He is now Managing Director of the ethical retail chain Out of This World.

Beyond public fundamentalism – a ministry in waiting
David Clark

A church, rooted in the Trinity and founded for the Kingdom, should be a blazing example of a learning community.

'THE CULT OF CERTAINTY'

We are a society spread-eagled between public arrogance and private anger (or exhaustion and helplessness if unemployment or homelessness is our lot). We live in a culture where to be certain, 'right', precocious and assertive is the hall-mark of the strong and the successful. To be uncertain, to be reflective and to be cautious is to be weak and inadequate. But this culture, a legacy of the 1980s, is set to wreak havoc in a world where we must live and work ever more closely together, or perish. For all our futures, public fundamentalism ('the cult of certainty') is a disaster.

We face disaster through economic fundamentalism. Monetarism may have fallen off its perch but 'the market', in language and liturgy, remains our god. The market allows, 'demands', 'decides' and cannot 'be bucked'. It is reified and deified in a way which dehumanizes all human transactions.

We face disaster through educational fundamentalism. That which is 'pro-gressive' and child-centred is trendy, self-indulgent and ineffective; that which is 'traditional' and subject-centred is safe and sound.

We face disaster through social fundamentalism. Gays and lesbians are not genuinely human beings, women are inadequate for roles, and to be over 50 (or redundant) is to have reached the end of one's useful life.

We face disaster through ethnic fundamentalism. We look with horror at the chaos tribalism has caused in Bosnia, South Africa or Northern Ireland. But back home racism of many kinds rumbles like an active volcano just below the surface.

Behind these and other forms of incestuous certainty lurks the fundamen-talism of politics. 'Thatcherism' and 'Statism' are but symbols of forces which pervade much of our political system and claim 'there is no alternative'. 'The reality is ...' trips from the lips in political debate after debate, as if we were not responsible for or could not challenge and change that 'reality'.

In religion too 'the truth' has not made us free but enslaved us. The tragedy is not so much that 'unity is dead' but that 'denominationalism reigns' en-trenched by dogmatism and inertia. And where old denominations are dying as an inevitable consequence, new ones, from 'moral majorities' to 'holy alliances', arise to perpetuate the deep divides – believing that calling ourselves 'non-denominational' makes us any less introverted than history's schismatics.

Fuelling this 'cult of certainty' is the magisterial authority of much of the press which only rarely puts its championing of 'righteousness' in inverted commas. 'Truth' is simple, obvious, unambiguous, indisputable, and only pub-lished by us! Everyone else is naïve, gullible, impractical, prudish, subversive or just plain daft.

Public fundamentalism is about gaining or retaining power and control. It breeds on past 'wrongs' and 'errors', real or mythical, seeking full reinstatement and reparation. But at its core lies a deep ambivalence – about meaning, purpose, worth and identity. Thus it seeks to put up the shutters, to close the doors. Its advocates are desperate to dominate, for true openness and exchange might weaken their cause, their image and their 'certainty'.

Public fundamentalism breeds on secrecy. It only communicates that which supports its own view of 'reality'. It thrives on ignorance, stereotypes and prejudice. It seeks to discredit research, enquiry and listening of an open-minded kind.

Public fundamentalism 'publishes to damn'. Its pronouncements about opponents are negative. 'Reality' is what we are and have; the rest is rubbished. It 'humanizes' its own people and party by dehumanizing others. It is 'us'; against 'them', or more often and more deadly, 'us' against 'it' (the inhuman enemy beyond the pale).

LEARNING COMMUNITIES

If public fundamentalism negates and divides, what can affirm and unite? In short, what is 'the human project' for the next millennium?

Such a project is, first and foremost, a process not a product. There is no 'blueprint' which can ensure the endurance of any society. Secondly, all 'economic miracles' depend on 'human miracles' or they remain a mirage. Thirdly, our situation demands both continuity and change, by itself the former stultifies and the latter exhausts.

This human project rests on two foundations – 'community' and 'learning' held together in a dynamic synthesis. The fashionable concept is 'synergy', wherein the whole becomes greater than the sum of the parts.

'Community' is a word urgently needing rehabilitation. Its reputation has been prostituted by overuse on the one hand and reactionary neglect on the other. But at root it is about *koinonia*, what we have in common as human beings. Community is that which makes us both unique as persons and one as people. Its (re)discovery holds the key to the future ... Community is about the continuity of life and living for all of us. Community embraces both the deeply personal and the richly interpersonal. It offers worth and dignity to the individual, integration and wholeness to the group. It gives people both a sense of significance, a part to play, and a sense of solidarity, a world to which to belong.

But a health warning! Community is hugely potent – the most powerful force known to humankind. Allowed to grow and strengthen along cultural boundaries it has immense potential to unite and energize. Kept caged by public fundamentalism its power becomes horrifically destructive. Aiding and abetting such captivity is the refusal to learn.

Those exploited by public fundamentalism know nothing of learning. They may be socialized into their culture or tradition. They gain knowledge through instruction and skills through training. But of genuine learning they are bereft. They remain circumscribed not only by history and territory, but by the closure of the mind to anything but the routine and the prescribed. 'Progress' is the dead of the past masquerading as the new – being 'radical' is not going back to one's roots in order to begin again but to return to the womb of the tribe or the clan.

To learn is to change – it is to take stock, to take risks and to take action. It is not to deny commitment or conviction but to use them as a springboard to new experiences, to discover new worlds and to make new friends. The 'subject–object' divide longer holds. Learning is an I–Thou or an I–You relationship, never an I–It one. Learning does not fit neatly into economic planning or national curriculums, into political manifestos or religious crusades. It is no quick fix. It is a slow, haphazard, cosy process just because it leads to real transformation.

Community depends on learning, and learning requires community. Continuity needs change, and change needs continuity. Public fundamentalism threatens both the continuity of community and learning to change. But without learning communities at the heart of our economic, educational, social, ethnic, political and religious life, we cannot begin to hope for 'the survival of the species'.

A MINISTRY IN WAITING

We are desperately short of genuine learning communities because we have few with the vision, the skill, the courage, the tenacity, the resources to promote and nourish them.

For communities to learn, frontiers must be opened, boundaries crossed and new encounters facilitated. Engagement has to be real and challenging, as well as secure and supportive. 'Community education' is an art far removed from the mundane practices which often take that name.

For communities to learn we need a host of 'mediating structures', 'intermediary agencies', to foster international, intercultural, intersector, interregional, interagency and interpersonal links. It is just such means of cross-fertilization that public fundamentalism is bent on negating and destroying.

For communities to learn we need a new 'profession' as yet only vaguely glimpsed by the powers that be in national and international affairs. Its features are at least fivefold. It is a ministry of affirmation – in which public fundamentalism is done away with by public recognition of the worth, the experience and the resources which each person and group possess. It is a ministry which refuses to label and stereotype. It is a ministry which works for alliances around common concerns and tasks. Its theme-song is about partnership and co-operation. It is a ministry which explores alternatives, because there always are different and diverse ways of being human. It fosters questioning, exploration and discovery. It is a ministry which seeks to prepare people for what gestalt psychologists call 'the Aha! experience' (what scientists might term 'enlightenment' and religious people 'conversion'). It is about 'double' and 'triple loop' learning, lateral shifts in perception and understanding which open new vistas and reveal fresh horizons. It is a ministry which leads to action in the form of sharing revelation and insights, of 're-presenting' the old made new and the ordinary discovered to be extraordinary.

A NEW ECUMENISM

To confront and overcome public fundamentalism, the destructive 'cult of certainty', is not a ministry in any way confined to Christians. 'The survival of the species' will depend on a vast multitude of 'creative connectors' of many faiths or none.

Yet a church, rooted in the Trinity and founded for the Kingdom, should be a blazing example of a learning community. If it is not such a body, crossing boundaries and overcoming divides, then for what does it exist? If it is not committed to a true 'ecumenism' – the transformation of the whole inhabited earth into a learning and loving community – of what earthly use is it? For such a church, praying that the Kingdom may come on earth as in heaven, this is 'a ministry in waiting'. 'The human project' and 'the divine project' require it.

Christian thought and action in public education
Jack Priestley

Christians in education today have a largely prophetic role. The vocabulary needs constantly to be challenged.

EDUCATION AND CENTRAL CONVICTIONS

Ernest Schumacher's classic book *Small Is Beautiful* (1973) is remembered most for its promotion of the idea of intermediate technology. However, its contents ranged far and wide and included a memorable and prophetic chapter on education which concluded:

> The problems of education are merely reflections of the deepest problems of our age. They cannot be solved by organization, administration or the expenditure of money even though the importance of all these is not denied. We are suffering from a metaphysical disease and the cure, therefore, must be metaphysical. Education which fails to clarify our central convictions is mere training or indulgence. For it is our central convictions which are in disorder and as long as the present anti-metaphysical temper persists the disease will grow worse.

In the twenty or so years since these words were written the disease has grown worse. Nor is this just a knee-jerk negative reaction to change. The anti-metaphysical temper to which Schumacher refers was, in his time, largely one of apathy. Now the very notion, not just of metaphysics, but of any theory at all is openly attacked. Teachers in training, we are told, should not have their time wasted on theory. What is needed is practical guidance on how to operate in the classroom.

This is asserted as if each were, in some way, mutually exclusive of the other. However, what we do in the classroom is derivative of what theory or theories we hold. It is theory which provides the basis for any profession. The hospital teacher who brought to an abrupt end a group conversation in a training college staff room with the question 'What do you tell your students about the education of dying children?' has a right to be answered. What indeed? The question cuts away at our current everyday assumptions:

- that the value of education lies only in the future;
- that that value has to do primarily with socio-economic factors;
- that the human being, like a car being put together on an assembly line, only has value when it is completed.

EDUCATION: WHAT IS IT FOR?

Religions have always laid claim to the deepest form of thinking about life, guardian as it were of the fundamental mystery of the depth of being from which all else emanates. This is why we cannot but respond to Schumacher's statement that 'Education which fails to clarify our central convictions is mere training or indulgence'. For the fact of the matter is, that there is precious little in the National Curriculum which has much to say about central convictions of any sort. The subject known as religious education, when it is taught well, attempts to fill that demand. But the very fact that it is placed outside the mainstream demonstrates for all to see the great irony that what is central for us as human beings is, in fact, for schools, regarded as peripheral.

'WHOEVER OWNS THE WORDS OWNS THE WORLD': WHO OWNS EDUCATIONAL LANGUAGE?

The key to the whole conflict between what Christians hold to be most important and how Christian teachers are expected to act in their public lives lies in language. The language of education is always parasitical. It does not have a special language of its own even if, back in the 1960s, certain educationists tried to invent a professional jargonese. For centuries the language of education was largely borrowed from religious life.

A school (from the Greek *scholē*) was a space where leisure was created in order to promote insight; in Western culture it derived from the monastic life of reading and contemplation. A college was a place based on fellowship and brotherhood.

Two things have changed in recent years. First, new dominant words and phrases have come into being largely from the language of business and commerce. Secondly, words which were largely the prerogative of religion have been reshaped and used in new contexts and, therefore, have acquired new meanings. Let us look at some examples and raise some relevant questions.

DOMINANT NEW LANGUAGE IN EDUCATION CONTEXTS

(a) State schools

In 1978, Shirley Williams, then Secretary of State for Education, declared in the midst of the Tameside dispute that she did not own a single school. They all belonged to Counties or to Voluntary Bodies (Churches). 'State schools' is now a common phrase. Could we have had a National Curriculum unless we had come to accept that our schools were national rather than local? Is a National Curriculum the same thing as a State Curriculum and why is one phrase used in preference to the other?

(b) Assessment, audit

We have always examined and made judgements about children and students. The words of commerce possess a far higher degree of objectivity. Are we making judgements about persons any more, or only judging what they know and what they can do? How much are we being pushed into giving high priority to that which can be easily assessed, and low priority to areas of human growth and development where objective assessment is difficult or impossible? Does this also lower the status of those curriculum areas such as art, music, and drama which contribute to our humanity rather than our skills or knowledge?

(c) Management

Schools used to have heads and teachers. They were led rather than managed. Now what was once the head's role has been taken away and divided up, first among Local Authority agencies, then increasingly by central Government. Vision is rarely called for. The head's job is to manage for someone else, and ideas of managing go right down the institution. Is a vicar a manager? Did Jesus manage the disciples? Is it enough to manage children? What does the common English phrase 'I can manage' imply?

TERMS ONCE REGARDED AS RELIGIOUS, NOW SECULARIZED

(a) Professional

Once heavy with the notion of service, this word has come to mean simply 'getting paid for it'. Is the defining characteristic of the professional the one whose first responsibility is to the client before all else? Is the client the child or the parent? What other characteristics make up the professional educator/teacher/academic?

(b) Vocationalism

Again the sense of service was until recently very strong. To have a vocation was to have a sense of being called. The word has been hijacked so that a vocational course is no more than a course directed to training for any job. Can one speak meaningfully of having a vocation to do most jobs?

(c) Mission

All institutions now produce mission statements. These are merely what a college, a school or a high street store exists to do. Most are in terms of profit. Less and less are they based on any ideal other than making money. The original idea of being sent has almost disappeared. Who decides the mission of a school?

Christians in education today have a largely prophetic role. The vocabulary needs constantly to be challenged. Beneath the words lies the metaphysic – a basic assumption of what the world and the people in it are, and what they exist for. The old metaphysics have died: new ones are being born. Christian educationalists should be at the forefront of the imaginative process of creating more meaningful language to describe what it is they are doing.

Jack Priestley has spent a professional lifetime working in religious education at all levels. Since 1991 he has been Principal of Westhill College of Higher Education, Birmingham.

Social work and public life

Howard Tripp

Churches have no right to abandon their role in the service of the needy, the marginalized, the weak and the handicapped.

'PUBLIC LIFE' AND 'PUBLIC SERVICE'

So often 'public life' was identified with Government and 'public service' with voluntary non-governmental activity. However, in more recent times, and especially since the advent of the Welfare State after the 1939–45 War, we have looked to Government not just to offer a framework for social work but to be a major provider of services. Whether we are about to see a change in this or not is a matter both of current speculation and concern. But we must always remember that the provision of care is as much an activity of public life as the making and enforcing of law.

Because initially so much of public service was provided by voluntary, and usually church, organizations, it is not surprising that there was and remains some competition and rivalry (as well as a good deal of co-operation) between what we call voluntary and statutory provision. But whether they are voluntary or statutory services, both must be acknowledged as genuine forms of public service.

PUBLIC LIFE FOR ALL

All this broadens considerably the concept of 'public life' and demands participation of many more in public life than just politicians and magistrates. In fact all need to be involved and should never relinquish their participation in our public life. It can be debated whether it is an innate human right that leads to democracy or simply the volume of tasks that demands the contribution of all. But it is clear that the contribution of all is demanded by economic necessity, if for no other reason than to provide the resources needed for the education, health and welfare of the whole nation.

Certainly public life must never be equated with a quinquennial visit to the polling booth and there casting, no matter how carefully studied, a vote. It demands a daily concern for the building up of a society that provides both a framework for the care and service of all, and the provision within that framework of those services called for not just by the taxpayer, but by objective standards of justice.

A NATIONALIZED SOCIAL SERVICE?

Subsidiarity and freedom would seem to encourage a combination of voluntary and statutory services to enhance the public good. Such a partnership also provides alternative ways of providing welfare. Citizens may contribute to social welfare either by paying taxes and voting for the welfare policies of particular party policies, or by offering their services and donations to particular voluntary organizations furthering their favoured policies.

It is said that voluntary organizations have greater freedom to initiate new work and new methods of work, whereas statutory initiatives are controlled and restricted by their close relationship with Government. The voluntary can be more localized and responsive while the statutory can be bureaucratically controlled and centrally circumscribed. Voluntary organizations can also provide competition which keeps the state providers on their toes. But as taxation has increased, voluntary organizations have found fund-raising more difficult and have frequently become more dependent upon Government. The result is that they are less challenging and adventurous and more likely to be pale reflections of statutory services.

. . .

THE CHRISTIAN MANDATE FOR PUBLIC SERVICE

The Christian churches have from the time of Christ played a special role in education, welfare and care. There are now those who would recommend that the state should take over these areas of public life directly. However it is not necessary that the state should do so and possibly threaten a new form of totalitarianism. What is necessary is that society should see that a public (but not necessarily a state) provision is made.

Further, churches have no right to abandon their role in the service of the needy, the marginalized, the weak or the handicapped. Their mandate flows not out of the needs of society but from the ordinances of their founder: 'So long as you did it to the least of my brethren you did it to me.' God has created the goods of this world for the use of all. Public service exists to make sure that these goods reach their universal destination and are not unfairly retained for the benefit of the few.

Many of us get caught up in public life and politics because of a deep social concern and a burning desire to improve the lot of some underprivileged group, or to see justice done for the less fortunate or marginalized members of society. This is one major route that leads to the vital engagement of Christians in Public Life.

The Right Reverend Howard Tripp is the Roman Catholic Auxiliary Bishop of Southwark.

Christian responses to a Health Service in transition

James Woodward

How can our theology guide and affirm individuals and groups working within the (Health) Service?

THE CONTEXT OF CHANGE

The National Health Service has undergone the most radical process of structural change since its creation in 1948 ... Few will disagree on the need for a change though the effects of the change on the Health Service are a matter of considerable debate and disagreement.

My overwhelming concern as a Chaplain in the Service is with the deep sense of crisis that both pervades health care institutions and professionals ... The pace and nature of this imposed change has sown the seeds of confusion, hostility and bitterness. This exhibits itself in widespread alienation of staff at all levels; particularly aimed at managers but also in a deep mistrust of politicians and, perhaps most alarmingly, in fears expressed by patients.

. . .

THEOLOGICAL PRINCIPLES GUIDING ACTION

In the light of this, how can our theology guide and affirm individuals and groups working within the Service?

Truth-telling

The most important theological principle that should guide our thought and action is that of struggling with the reality of the truth as we perceive it. This principle should encourage and affirm our sharing of the conflicts, ambiguities and limitations that we experience in and around us. In particular, it should encourage us to be explicit about the values that we believe to undergird the Health Service and especially the values from which we feel removed and alienated. There are always positive opportunities to be grasped during change and the changes within the Health Service are no exception to this.

The limits to care

Part of the impetus for change has been driven by both financial constraints and the general public's ever expanding expectations around health. Is it realistic to expect that all our needs for health can be funded through a tax-funded service? What are the limits to care? The theological truth here is about human dignity as against human transience. That is, is it a moral absolute and a basic human right (in view of our mortality) that we should have life prolonged at any cost?

Trans-national equity

While discussing this within our own context, there are important issues about trans-national equity. What are we to make of our relative medical luxury in Europe in comparison to extreme deprivation in parts of the Third World? Such issues as these flow from a sense of basic concepts regarding the human being as a creature of God within the created order and one whose destiny is not confined to material flourishing at any cost. There is always, however hard, an eschatological dimension: a sense of the 'more' and the 'other'.

Market in health-care

There are some important questions to be asked about the concept of the market in health care. Can health really be treated as a commodity in the world of business and commerce? Surely the labelling of people as 'customers' degrades everyone to a means in a market, rather than ends in caring and creative institutions? How far does the cost accounting performed in the name of efficiency and the targeting of resources (albeit proper and essential aims in the functioning of any institutions) result in human interchanges being dominated by finance and accounting instead of human accountability? Does this process down-grade patients only to units of consumption and treatment? How does the technical enterprise of health care relate to the human dimensions of care? These are difficult but fundamental theological questions, ultimately about God and the nature of humanity.

WHAT CAN BE DONE? SOME PASTORAL STRATEGIES

There are important steps which we can all take within our own immediate environment which contribute towards changing the general culture around us and equipping us to respond creatively and constructively to change.

Staff support

We need to encourage health care organizations to put staff support on its agenda. We need to think about the way in which we support our colleagues. This is about promoting the ethos that support is for everybody and that needing support is not an admission of weakness but declaration of strength and evidence of insight.

Using our Christian resources

From a Christian perspective we need to continue to articulate the dilemmas and ambiguities of our present situation. How do Christians cope with change? How does our theology support and affirm us in our place of work?

Training and education

The above is part of ensuring that training and education should always include aspects of self-development and self-awareness.

Rethinking change?

When an organization is changing, we do have a unique opportunity to promote change by helping others to rethink established customs. We do not necessarily need always to do something in the way that it has always been done in the past.

Caring for ourselves

Above all, we need to look at our own lifestyle and the quality of our life to ensure that we care for ourselves adequately. The principle here is that improvement in our own lifestyle may well improve the quality of living for those around us.

James Woodward was formerly Anglican Chaplain in The Queen Elizabeth Hospital, Birmingham. He is now parish priest of Middleton and Wishaw, and Bishop's Adviser for Health and Social Care in the Diocese of Birmingham.

Forgiveness in public life

Brian Frost

Forgiveness lies at the heart of our liberation.

FORGIVENESS AND 'JUSTICE'

When discussions are held about forgiveness in public life people often concede there is something in the idea – even recognize that there are instances where this has occurred. But they want to know how such a concept relates to justice, to repentance and reparation, as well as to reconciliation and to love. This is a thorny area, especially for Christians, not least because the New Testament and its ethics suggest that on occasions Jesus saw forgiveness to be independent of repentance. At the same time, the Lord's Prayer itself seems to contain a threat: if we do not forgive, we will not be forgiven.

Is there any way through this seeming jungle? Perhaps only if we appreciate that true justice always includes some element of forgiveness as one of its crucial ingredients, even if that forgiveness does not always evoke repentance. Jesus from the Cross uttered words of forgiveness but there is no indication there was any response.

. . .

FORGIVENESS IN BRITISH LIFE

Can anything be said about forgiveness in the public life of Britain? There are many situations needing this balm. Take the eight hundred years of Britain's involvement with Ireland, for example, and now such a complex tangle it seems it can never be made right. What ought to be done? Perhaps we can learn from post-war Germany. Then Pastor Niemöller and others issued a statement, called the Stuttgart Declaration, which acknowledged German responsibility for the suffering the war had caused. Others in Germany attacked it, saying nations besides Germany had a responsibility, too. Niemöller and his colleagues remained adamant. They were clear that Germany had to accept responsibility for what as a nation it had done.

What, one wonders, could happen between Britain and Ireland if leading figures in Britain were to issue a declaration similar to the Stuttgart one? Of course there would be the need for an Irish Stuttgart Declaration, too. But that is not Britain's responsibility. We have a responsibility on this island to come to terms with *our* history and *our* sins.

A contemporary matter in the public life of Britain involving forgiveness is the situation of the Royal Family. Here is a forgiveness issue on another complex scale. Few know all the truth. Have we, as a society, failed the Royal Family by our appetite for 'scandal'? Have they failed us, and need our forgiveness? ...

A more earthly matter is the relationship of the police with the community. Do we need more public discussion about what we expect of the police and how we treat them as a body? Like us they are fallible. But are there not tremendous burdens on them? Are our procedures for handling the situations that arise where there is failure adequate enough?

Finally, can the churches help? In our divided state we are not exactly shining examples of forgiveness and reconciliation. Things are better between us now than before. Yet we still have a long way to go. Can we be taken really seriously until we get our act together and genuinely unite? If the essence of Christianity is that fallible, sinning people are forgiven and brought into a new fellowship with each other and the world then we have to prove it or live a lie.

Forgiveness lies at the heart of our liberation. Without it reconciliation, at whatever level, becomes arid and withers. Justice without forgiveness leaves a bitter taste in the mouth and love becomes sentimentality.

Brian Frost is the author of *The Politics of Peace*, a study of forgiveness in public life in many parts of the world during this century (Darton, Longman & Todd, 1991), and *Women and Forgiveness* (Collins, Fontana, 1990). He is more recently author of the biography of Donald Soper, *Goodwill on Fire* (Hodder and Stoughton, 1995).

Conclusion

David Clark

Our Introduction took the story of the churches' most recent attempts to engage collectively with the public arena up to the launch of Christians in Public Life (CIPL) early in 1992. At that moment in time there was some optimism that the slow drift towards the privatization of faith over recent decades could be reversed. But the later 1990s sees that optimism giving way, not so much to pessimism as to a realization that the birth of a new kind of church fit and able to bring faith to bear on daily life in any authentic and coherent way is going to be a long and painful process.

AMBIGUOUS SIGNALS

The late 1980s and first half of the 1990s did see some interesting initiatives, albeit on a very limited budget, coming to the fore. Three of these were based in Cambridge. In 1983, the Jubilee Centre, a Christian research and campaigning organization, with a growing focus on a relational philosophy rooted in Christian principles, was set up. In 1987, the Von Hügel Institute was established at St Edmund College as a professional Roman Catholic research centre for the interdisciplinary study of Christianity and society. Two years later, down the road at Ridley Hall, the Ridley Hall Foundation came into being (originally called the 'God on Monday' project) to help Christians relate faith to the world of business, this time with a more evangelical theology to the fore.

In 1993, MODEM (Managerial and Organizational Disciplines for the Enhancement of Ministry) was founded, emerging from the demise, and taking forward the work, of the old CORAT (the Christian Organizations Research and Advisory Trust, set up in 1968). MODEM's aim is to facilitate an exchange of managerial and organizational skills between the work place and the churches. In the same year, CHRISM (CHRistians In Secular Ministries) came into being to give organizational form to a hitherto loose network of Anglican MSEs (ministers in secular employment), the new association purposefully committing itself to an ecumenical membership. In the meantime, longer established bodies like the William Temple Foundation (set up in 1971) and the Institute for Contemporary Christianity (established in 1982) continued to develop their ministries in new and creative ways.

However, there were powerful forces working in a contrary direction, not least the decline of the mainstream churches' economic resources (including those of the Church of England), which were bringing about a significant amount of 'downsizing'. The biannual conference of the Industrial Mission Association, held in March 1996, was pointedly called 'Changing Gear'. Despite many signs of renewed commitment to the industrial mission ideal, there was quite clearly more than modest concern about the termination of the contracts of industrial missioners in certain dioceses, and the increasing trend towards part-time appointments almost everywhere. In 1996, the long-established Industry Churches Forum (formerly the Industrial Christian Fellowship) reported the termination of the roles of its Director and Secretary, and indicated that its future was now in jeopardy. At the same time, it was announced that Methodism's Luton Industrial College, established in the 1950s, was to close, with its work being put on a peripatetic basis under the title of 'Mission in Business, Industry and Commerce'.

Overall, therefore, despite the exhortatory spate of denominational reports and two major conferences on public affairs which characterized the late 1980s and early 1990s (see the Introduction), and in spite of the emergence of a number of new organizations or centres committed to faith and daily life issues, the turn of the millennium sees the church in England still struggling to find the means and the mode of giving impetus and shape to its effective engagement with the public arena. So what of the future?

A NEW MEDIUM

One thing is certain, as all the papers appearing in this book show: that the public issues facing humankind in the years to come will be as momentous as any that have occurred hitherto. The twentieth century has been one of phenomenal change with few signs of the pace of that change decelerating as we cross the millennial threshold. Never are creative, redemptive and caring institutions more needed to offer inspiration and hope to a society often bemused and bewildered by the rapid destruction of old landmarks, physical, economic, ethical and religious. Never do human beings need more to find a way of affirming and sustaining their common humanity in the face of the polar foes of fragmentation and fundamentalism.

The Christian church has much to learn – but it also has an immense amount to offer our volatile world. The church is still a power-house for the salvation and fulfilment of humankind. Its message, spelt out across all these papers, is as indispensable now as ever it was, with the Trinity and the Kingdom prime theological paradigms for our time. Christ's call for us to become fully human and fully human together has never been more relevant. These papers argue cogently for that potent message to be more clearly identified, clarified and communicated, not for the sake of the few but for the sake of all.

But the message needs a medium which both personifies and promotes it. It requires a church shaped and equipped for its task in this and succeeding generations. It needs an institution which treasures but learns from its past, which can keep the faith with passion but re-present its message with imagination, ingenuity and intelligence.

These papers begin to sketch out an agenda for such a church in the public realm in the next century; but that agenda has to begin to be made a reality *now*. So in this concluding part we outline some of the key features of that agenda and offer a few suggestion as to how the latter might begin to take practical shape.

THE NATIONAL SCENE

Different denominations have different views of the church as an institution. The picture is highly diverse and complex as those working ecumenically at the national level know only too well (see *Called to be One*, 1996). However, the trend over recent decades in all denominations has been to 'downsize' organizationally at national level, and to hope that the regional and especially local expressions of church will take the strain. The dominant impetus for this comes from two quarters: the conviction that 'subsidiarity' (decision-making delegated to those most immediately affected) is now the name of the game and, more realistic and influential, economic decline. At the same time, the pro-active British Council of Churches has disappeared, with the more skeletal and less publicly vocal Council of Churches for Britain and Ireland (and regional equivalents) taking its place.

As a consequence, and in the light of many points made in these papers, therefore, it must be asked whether the church as a national institution is in danger of neglecting one of its primary tasks. For if public life is to be addressed in any effective way, then there are certain things which the church at national level can and must do better than anyone else. The churches nationally, for example, have a vitally important advocacy role with government and other secular institutions. Only national denominational leaders can gain the ear of other national leaders across all sectors. What such church leaders say and when they say it is of considerable significance for other Christians in public life across the country. If the former fail to fulfil this task, the repercussions reverberate right 'down' the system to the local level. Criticism and advocacy must continue to be undertaken nationally with professional skill and proper resources.

However, the church as a national advocate or critic has to be aware of its changing status. Dogmatic pronouncements 'from on high' are now a nonsense. The day is long gone when people listened with bated breath for church leaders to pronounce on this or that contemporary issue. The 'authority' of any statement now depends as much on well researched argument as on who makes it. Nor does ecclesiastical consensus *per se* add very much weight.

What is in fact most wanting in public life today is for national church leaders to promote open and honest dialogue. They need to move beyond the current obsession with lists of 'noble values'. Whilst being candid about the Christian convictions which motivate them, they should be actively encouraging real debate amongst those of differing convictions and viewpoints. Championing such an open-ended approach would be an immense asset in setting the agenda and the style for the all-important debate which needs to take place between Christians and non-Christians in public life at every level and across all sectors. It is a stance which would immediately legitimize the concept of 'mission as dialogue' advocated in several of our papers, and help to bridge the divide between a church and a society so often failing to listen to and learn from one another.

Although church leaders at national level have this vital role to play, however, it should be more fully recognized that they are not the only channels through which the views of 'the church' can or should be made public. Thus church leaders and church bodies 'at the centre' should be doing their utmost to promote the expression of Christian convictions in the public sphere, formally or informally, at all levels. If there is an expectation that the (largely clerical) denominational agencies will 'speak for the whole church', local and regional commentary, not least that by informed laity, will be all too often devalued.

To espouse a new national commitment to promote dialogue not dogmatism, and to foster the expression of Christian convictions at every level of church life, will necessitate a re-shaping of ecclesiastical structures. If this does not occur, public engagement which might happen at regional or local level will be, at best, inhibited and, at worst, stifled.

Few of the papers in this book explicitly address the organization and operation of the churches at national level. But, taken together with CIPL's *Survey of Christians at Work* (Clark, 1993), the pointers are clear. Some ongoing means of national networking to support all Christians active in the public arena is urgently needed. The Christians in Public Life Programme has more recently blazed a trail, and other bodies and centres have at one time or another made a significant contribution to this concern. But a national initiative by the churches working together is now imperative to repair this gaping hole in current missionary strategy.

An ongoing national network for Christians in public life would have a number of characteristics. It would be formally and actively supported by the national churches. The focus would be lay vocation in the public arena. The approach would be *inclusive* – across every sector (education, health, industry, government, etc.) as far as society is involved; *ecumenical* as far as the church is concerned. There would be a national 'resource unit' to focus, promote and sustain the network. This would be responsible for the collection and dissemination of information and comment through a wide diversity of channels, not least using the new information technologies.

There would be an ecumenical team of pro-active catalysts regionally based across the whole country to develop and sustain such a network. These 'animateurs' would be a key link between the local, regional and national scenes (see below). This is skilled work and those involved would need specialized training and proper resourcing. The churches, in order to make maximum use of such a network, would set up regular regional and national forums on current issues of significance. One such national event would be along the lines of the German Kirchentag, adapted to suit the cultural context of the UK.

THE REGIONAL SCENE

If it is the task of the church nationally to provide a framework to promote and sustain the vocation of all Christians in public life, it is the responsibility of the church regionally to make this missionary undertaking a practical reality.

No effective mission to public life can be undertaken at regional level until the most significant socio-geographic areas for engagement have been identified. As long ago as the 1950s, Canon Boulard, the French sociologist, gave the name *zone humaine* to such regions (Boulard, 1960). In our day and age, with the increasing dispersal of power not only nationally but globally, identifying these natural groupings has become more complex. But the *zone humaine* still remains a very important concept for Christian mission.

Many of the theological and organizational principles suggested above for the church at national level would be reflected in any regional missionary structure. Here, however, we draw attention to three particularly important structural requirements (see also Clark, 1984, pp. 158–64; Clark, 1988, pp. 9–19; Clark, 1996b, pp. 31–4).

Sector networks and groups

We have already employed the term 'sectors' to refer to those major aspects of institutional life (education, health, welfare, industry and commerce, law and order, government and so forth) which dominate the public scene. Christian mission in the public domain has to take engagement with such sectors within regional (as well as national) life very seriously. There are other focuses of mission – the neighbourhood for one. But if the church does not pay as much attention to the ministry of its lay people in the sectors as it does to neighbourhood life, then it will become increasingly marginalized.

Just as effective mission depends on the clear identification of the *zone humaine*, it also depends on thoughtful and sustained engagement with key sectors of regional life. One way forward here (Clark, 1996b, pp. 31–4) is for a person closely in touch with and well informed about the sector concerned to be designated as a 'contact' or 'link person' for that sector. Their main role in this context would be to promote networks and groups of Christians within these sectors, and to explore ways by which these could be nurtured, developed and sustained within a vocational context. Such groups and networks would be neither holy huddles nor humanistic debating societies, but the means of enabling Christians in public life to engage faithfully and openly as Christians with the many challenges presented by the sector within which they were set.

We say more below about the profile of these link persons. Here we simply point out that this role could be the heart of an innovative form of ordained ministry. That those pioneering this role are currently being withdrawn from sector responsibilities, or (as with ministers in secular employment) their ministry therein given minimal affirmation, is symptomatic of our current obsession with maintaining past structures and neglecting new ones.

Assemblies

If the holistic nature of the ministry of Christians in public life is to be kept to the fore, it is not enough for the church to operate only within the more service orientated sectors. There must be a recognition of the totality and interdependence of the *zone humaine*.

This might be achieved in numerous ways. One is the holding of occasional assemblies which bring Christians together from across an entire *zone humaine* to exchange experiences, concerns and insights about their public vocation. Such a gathering would be very different from a synod – so often dominated by an ecclesiastical agenda. Acknowledged Christian centres, such as cathedrals, might play a prominent role here.

Resource centre

The ministry of Christians within the sectors of the *zone humaine* needs a focal point, to facilitate meeting and resourcing. This might take the form of a resource centre which would embrace a database of Christian personnel and projects, as well as briefing material relating to the vocational and ethical concerns arising in different sectors. The centre would also be a focus for research and training.

How the details of these three aspects of Christian ministry in public life (networks and groups, assemblies and a resource centre) were worked out in any particular region would be a matter dependent on the character and culture of the region concerned. There are many variations on the theme – from involvement with centres for theological training, to partnerships with secular and other faith agencies addressing similar concerns. But the key factor is the commitment to a new way of being church for the sake of furthering the Kingdom in the *zone humaine*.

THE LOCAL SCENE

If the thrust of what has been suggested above begins to reshape the form of the church's institutional engagement with society at national and regional level, it will have major implications for the local church. A good number of our papers have specifically addressed this matter. Not least, such a change of priorities at local level might at last begin to reverse the low rating given by Christians at work (Clark, 1993) to the support given them from that quarter.

It is our contention that if the local congregation were able to embrace the ministry of its members in public life as an integral part of a wider enterprise, actively affirmed and resourced by the church at national and regional level in practical and explicit ways, then new meaning and purpose would be given to the whole of that congregation's ministry. It is because the local church is so often left to fend for itself, out on a limb and unable to discern any collective relevance beyond the family and neighbourhood, that its crucial role of offering sustenance and encouragement to its members in their public lives is either ignored or undeveloped.

Nothing could be more important than offering Christians in public life opportunities for the kind of worship which values and enriches their vocation in the cut and thrust of the public arena. Nothing is more essential for such ambassadors of the faith as pastoral care which appreciates and responds to their vocational concerns. Nothing is more vital for those constantly facing decisions where ethical considerations are so often confused, than the chance to reflect on and discuss these matters in an educationally and spiritually enlightening context. Nothing is more essential for such Christians as a local church which offers communal interest in and support for their tough missionary calling.

A local church which moves in this direction does not end up draining its energies but increasing them. The young are offered new role models of what it means to be a Christian in the public domain – warts and all. The old are given the chance of being kept in touch with a rapidly changing world, and of being able to offer their hard-won wisdom and larger perspectives to the debate. A local congregation which 'goes public' is not moving beyond its brief, but enhancing all aspects of its life by responding to the whole not a part of what Christian vocation means in today's world. The problem is not that 'our God is too small' but that 'our church is too small'. Because we have ceased to expect much of the local church, we have ceased to gain much from it. Our congregations are not just becoming congregations of 'the Third Age', but congregations of the Third Age with their potential contribution to public life ignored.

The church at local level needs to take its missionary task in the public domain into the *whole* of its life for *all* of its members. This means that it must be open to change. It cannot be held to ransom by clergy or laity who wish to preserve it as a religious club for those whose faith has been domesticated or privatized, a place of comfort but not of challenge.

The hall-mark of the kind of local church which we are describing here is that it becomes 'a learning community' in the deepest and fullest sense of that concept (Clark, 1996a, 1996b). The local congregation has to become a microcosm of what true community is all about, not least in the public domain. It needs to embrace, with commitment and excitement, the idea that to be the church in the world is to be on a steep learning curve. The latter is a result not only of a rapidly changing society, but also of what God is doing and where he is leading all of us at the outset of a new millennium.

CRITICAL FACTORS

For the Christian church to 're-form' itself in anything like the way suggested here, two factors are of critical importance – a renewed commitment to ecumenism on the one hand, and a search for innovative forms of leadership on the other.

The ecumenical dimension

The churches have now played hide and seek with ecumenism for nearly a century, if we take the missionary conference in Edinburgh in 1910 to be the launch-pad of the 'modern' ecumenical movement in this land. The disheartening thing is not that progress has been so slow. Indeed on the local level some impressive advances are in evidence (*Called to be One*, 1996). The disturbing fact is that the passion has ebbed away. It no longer seems to matter very much that the churches have redundant plant, tired ministers and are witnessing the proliferation of yet more 'denominations' amongst the black churches and within the independent 'house church' movement.

In the next millennium the church has to tackle the issue of genuine ecumenism with new zeal and determination or it will simply give added weight to the fragmentation of an already fragmented world. But the way forward is not to become again pre-occupied with 'faith and order'. It is to look more avidly at its mission to further the business of the Kingdom in public life. In reality, such a mission to public life cannot any longer be effectively promoted, not even for an established Church of England, on a denominational basis. A new ecumenical initiative is utterly essential to the church's re-engagement with the public domain. The transformation of society depends on it; the renewal of the church is conditional on it.

The local church as it is cannot go much further. It will remain corralled by wider constraints until the church at national and regional level gets its ecumenical act together. A fresh initiative empowered by courageous risk-taking is now imperative. There must be a determined attempt to overcome the ecumenical inertia which is increasingly draining the whole church of purpose, passion and people.

There are signs of hope, however, particularly at regional level. A trail has been blazed on the Merseyside scene with the setting up of the Merseyside and Region Churches' Ecumenical Assembly in 1985. This initiative must not be viewed as a one-off brainchild of a few charismatic church leaders. Despite inevitable limitations, it should be promoted and developed as a foretaste of things to come. The Churches Commission in the North East (Beales, *IM Agenda*, May 1996, pp. 5–6), a consortium of church bodies concerned with the Christian contribution to the public life of that region, has since 1996 also been breaking new ground. And CIPL's Human City Initiative, launched in Birmingham in 1995 (Clark, 1996b), is providing another possible model for the future. Other moves of a similar, though more limited, kind are in evidence in Nottinghamshire and Derbyshire, in Staffordshire and in Essex, as well as in Milton Keynes (*Called to be One*, 1996). In all such endeavours, it is the commitment to transform society and not just the church that is the key to the emergence of a new and dynamic ecumenical movement.

Leadership

We have left the issue of leadership till last because it lies at the heart of the church's discovery of a new and public mode of mission. From all that has been said above, it will be evident that real change has come about where leaders have had vision, courage and tenacity. Of course 'the laity' forms the essential core of the church as a missionary endeavour. But the leadership, and this must in institutional terms largely mean the clergy, can either inspire or kill that endeavour. It is high time to recognize what is common knowledge in every other kind of organization from businesses to schools: that quality of leadership is the critical factor.

The challenge for the mission of the church in public life in the next millennium is to find national and regional leaders who can enable it to flourish in a new era. Such leadership will be not so much a matter of personality as of style. It will be one which promotes and fosters the exercise of lay vocation in the public arena through new and imaginative organizational practices; pastoral, educational, communal. The hall-mark of this kind of leadership will be the ability to inspire, catalyse and co-ordinate the public and ecumenical expression of the church's mission. It will in effect be a new form of *episcopē*.

Within the more specialized sector (secular institutional) context, leadership might well be characterized by the following functions (Clark, 1986):

- discerning and interpreting the signs of the Kingdom;
- identifying and being alongside Christians in secular institutions;
- encouraging a sense of 'authentic secular vocation' amongst the people of God;
- gathering the church into vocational networks and groups;
- facilitating prayer and reflection in relation to the signs of the Kingdom and the response that these are requiring;
- offering the established means of grace as and when needed, but pointing up 'secular sacraments' of the Kingdom;
- pastorally supporting and resourcing Christians in this context;
- calling the people of God to account, positively not inspectorially;
- 'holding the circle' by ensuring that each network and group recognizes itself as part of the wider whole;
- taking occasional personal initiatives, but only to 'point the way'.

It should be noted here that the role outlined is very different from that of the traditional chaplain whose primary concern has usually been pastoral, and whose focus has been on 'the church in the workplace' rather than the transformation of institutions. What is now needed is a lateral shift in our understanding of what 'sector ministry' is all about.

The nature of the leadership of local congregations will also need radical reappraisal. If the public dimension of Christian mission is to be integrated into congregational life as indicated above, ministers will need to be re-equipped for this new 'professional' task. Such a role is not one that can be undertaken successfully by a mere change of heart. It will require fresh skills for the conduct of worship, in relation to pastoral care as well as education. It will demand acquaintance with the still ill-explored area of 'applied theology', and with the widely neglected field of Christian ethics. It will necessitate the acquiring of management and group work experience. In short, it will require not one person but a team approach through which the skills needed can be adequately provided.

All this has major implications for the training of clergy. If the ministry as a second career is becoming the norm (and there are grave problems with this for the church as a risk-taking community), then at least the previous experience of ordinands should not be left at the theological college gate. The future preparation of clergy will need a new curriculum if the public mission of the congregation is not to be stifled by a parochial form of ordained leadership – male or female.

CHANGING WORLD

It could be argued that this concluding chapter falls into the very trap that this book has attempted to avoid: pre-occupation with the church.

There is indeed another book to be written about just how the agenda set out in these papers, and in this last chapter, might work itself out in the life of our society. To that end, CIPL's Human City Initiative, underway since early 1995, has published many papers (only a few of which have been included here) focused on the practical contribution of the church to an urban world. That story must continue to be told, reflected on and responded to, for the transformation of our world not the transformation of any church is the ultimate goal.

Yet without the latter's 're-formation', a changing world will leave in its wake an unchanging church, and be all the more impoverished for that. If this is God's world and his Kingdom is to come on earth, then the church with all its failings remains an immensely important channel of his grace. It was never God's will that his people should become redundant. To neglect the public mission of Christians in a pluralistic age, or to relativize and downgrade that ministry, is simply to play the world's game. Beliefs matter, faith is important, hope is vital, without love wealth is worthless. The church exists to witness to what God's gift of the fullness of human life, personal and public, really means. For the salvation of a changing world, a changing church is a divine imperative.

References

All Are Called: Towards a Theology of the Laity (1985). London: Church Information Office.

Allen, R. (3 Nov. 1995) Book review 'How deep is ecology?', *The Times Higher Educational Supplement.* London.

Bagshaw, P. (1994) *The Church Beyond the Church.* Sheffield: Industrial Mission in South Yorkshire.

Beales, C. (May 1996) 'The Churches Regional Commission in the NE', *Industrial Mission Association Agenda.* Great Yarmouth: Industrial Mission Association.

Bonhoeffer, D. (1953) *Letters and Papers from Prison.* London: SCM Press.

Boulard, F. (1960) *An Introduction to Religious Sociology,* trans. M. J. Jackson. London: Darton, Longman & Todd.

Brierley, P. and Wraight, H. (eds) (1995) *UK Christian Handbook.* London: Christian Research.

Buber, M. (1958; first published 1937) *I and Thou.* 2nd edn. Edinburgh: T. & T. Clark.

Called to be Adult Disciples (1987). London: General Synod Board of Education.

Called to be One (1996). London: Churches Together in England.

Christifideles Laici (1989) Simplified version. Pinner: The Grail.

Clark, D. (1984) *The Liberation of the Church.* Westhill College, Birmingham: National Association of Christian Communities and Networks.

Clark, D. (1986) 'An examination of sector ordained ministry in response to "The Ministry of the People of God" (A report to the Methodist Conference, June 1986)'. Birmingham: unpublished paper.

Clark, D. (1987) *Yes to Life.* London: Collins (Fount Paperback).

Clark, D. (1988) *What Future for Methodism?* Westhill College, Birmingham: The Harborne Group.

Clark, D. (1993) (ed.) *A Survey of Christians at Work.* Westhill College, Birmingham: CIPL.

Clark, D. (1996a) *Schools as Learning Communities: Transforming Education.* London: Cassell.

Clark, D. (1996b) *The Communal Imperative.* Westhill College, Birmingham: CIPL.

Cox, H. (1965) *The Secular City.* London: SCM Press.

Dulles, A. (1974) *Models of the Church.* Dublin: Gill & Macmillan.

Echlin, E. P. (1989) *The Christian Green Heritage: World as Creation.* Cambridge: Grove Booklets.

Echlin, E. P. (1992) *The Deacon and Creation*. London: The Church Union.

Elliott, C. (1988) *Signs of Our Times*. Basingstoke: Marshall Pickering.

Faith in the City (1985). London: Church House Publishing.

Frost, B. (1991) *The Politics of Peace*. London: Darton, Longman & Todd.

Gibbs, M. and Morton, R. T. (1964) *God's Frozen People*. London: Collins Fontana.

Gibbs, M. and Morton. R. T. (1971) *God's Lively People*. London: Collins Fontana.

Gilbert, A. D. (1980) *The Making of Post-Christian Britain*. London: Longman.

Gilligan, C. (1982) *In a Different Voice?* Cambridge, MA: Harvard University Press.

Goodwin, R. (1991) *Living in the Fast Lane*. Peterborough: Methodist Publishing House.

Grant, G. (1986) *Technology and Justice*. Ontario: Anansi Press.

Grey, M. (1989) *Redeeming the Dream*. London: SPCK.

Handy, C. (1990) *The Age of Reason*. London: Arrow Books.

Harrison, M. (1995) *Visions of Heaven and Hell*. London: Channel 4 Television, Broadcasting Support Services.

Hastings, A. (1991) 3rd edn. *A History of English Christianity 1920–1990*. London: SCM Press.

Haughton, R. (1981) *The Passionate God*. London: Darton, Longman & Todd.

Heyward, C. (1984) 'Blessing the Bread: a Litany' in *Our Passion for Justice*. New York: Pilgrim.

Hughes, G. W. (1985) *God of Surprises*. London: Darton, Longman & Todd.

Industrial Mission: An Appraisal (1988). London: Board for Social Responsibility, Church House.

The Iona Community (1991) *Worship Book*. Glasgow: Wild Goose Publications.

Jenkins, D. (1988) *God, Jesus and Life in the Spirit*. London: SCM Press.

Küng, H. (1978) *On Being a Christian*. London: Collins, Fount.

Lebacqz, K. (1987) *Justice in an Unjust World*. Minneapolis: Augsburg Publishing House.

McFadyen, A. (1990) *The Call to Personhood*. Cambridge: Cambridge University Press.

Marquand, D. (1988) *The Unprincipled Society*. London: Cape

The Ministry of the People of God in the World (1990). Report to the Methodist Conference. Peterborough: Methodist Publishing House.

Munson, J. (1991) *The Nonconformists*. London: SPCK.

Newbigin, L. (1983) *The Other Side of 1984*. Geneva: World Council of Churches.

Newbigin, L. (1989) *The Gospel in a Pluralist Society*. London: SPCK.

Niles, P. (1989) *Resisting the Threats of Life*. Geneva: World Council of Churches.

Oppenheimer, H. (1983) *The Hope of Happiness*. London: SCM Press.

Oppenheimer, H. (1995) 'Mattering', *Studies in Christian Ethics*, vol. 8, no. 1. Edinburgh: T. & T. Clark.

Palmer, P. (1977) *A Place Called Community*. Pennsylvania: Pendle Hill.

Palmer, P. (1991; first published 1981) *The Company of Strangers: Christians and the Renewal of America's Public Life*. New York: Crossroad.

Schumacher, E. (1973) *Small Is Beautiful*. London: Blond and Briggs.

Schüssler-Fiorenza, E. (1992) *But She Said: Feminist Practices of Biblical Interpretation*. Boston: Beacon.

Tutu, D. (1983) *Hope and Suffering*. Grand Rapids: Eerdmans.

Vanstone, W. H. (1982) *The Stature of Waiting*. London: Darton, Longman & Todd.

Vaughan, P. H. (1990) *Non-Stipendiary Ministry in the Church of England*. San Francisco: Mellen Research University Press.

Welch, S. (1990) *A Feminist Ethic of Risk*. Minneapolis: Fortress.

Williams, C. (1963) *Where in the World?* New York: National Council of the Churches of Christ.

Williams, C. (1964) *What in the World?* New York: National Council of the Churches of Christ.

Williams, R. (1996) 'God and risk (2)' in R. Holloway (ed.), *The Divine Risk*. London: Darton, Longman & Todd.